Rhymes in Me

Giridhar Jaded

AuthorReputationPress
Creativity & Branding

*GOOD KARMA
KINDNESS IS FREE*

Copyright © 2019 by Giridhar Jaded.

All rights reserved. No part of this publication may be reproduced, distributed, or transmitted in any form or by any means, including photocopying, recording, or other electronic or mechanical methods, without the prior written permission of the publisher, except in the case of brief quotations embodied in critical reviews and certain other noncommercial uses permitted by copyright law. For permission requests, write to the publisher, addressed "Attention: Permissions Coordinator," at the address below.

Author Reputation Press LLC
45 Dan Road Suite 36
Canton MA 02021
www.authorreputationpress.com
Hotline: 1(800) 220-7660
Fax: 1(855) 752-6001

Ordering Information:
Quantity sales. Special discounts are available on quantity purchases by corporations, associations, and others. For details, contact the publisher at the address above.

Printed in the United States of America.

ISBN-13:   Softcover   978-1-951727-58-1
           eBook   978-1-951727-59-8

Library of Congress Control Number: pending

Dedication Page

A photo on my living room wall,
Makes the place feel like home,
A picture of two different times,
Made into one for lack of time,
To be captured posing together,
A photo of my Mother & my Father,
Who left me in that very order.
But made me enough of a fighter,
To live a life of kindness, for it matters,
You are with me, without being with me,
You did enough to let me be a better me.
My first book is an offering at your feet,
On a journey new, Mom & Dad, your blessings, all I seek.

Contents

A Guitar 1
Words Are All I Have 2
A Salute to Law Enforcement 3
Will You Be My Valentine? 4
Patience 5
Love of Old Times 6
The Art of Meditation 8
Something about you 9
The bygone winter 10
Memories worth making 11
A distant country 12
The demons inside me 13
My renaissance song 14
Have a joyful ride 15
A little more alive 16
Blinking eyes 17
Lost in Your Brown Hues 18
Gratitude filled kiss 19
2:00 AM thoughts 20
The Poetry in You 21
Smiles Are Free 22
You by my side 23
The Birds in Words 24
Say No to wasting food 25
People that matter 26
To Love or Be Loved? 27
A careless world 28
A winter morning run 29
Take good care of your Life 30
Trolling 31
Love Your Demeanor 32
Healthy Living 33

TGIF	34
Moments of pure bliss	35
Just let it be	36
Art Rocks	37
Continue Being in Love	38
Technology's pangs	39
A goodnight kiss	40
You Score A 9 Out of 10	41
Love spell	42
A chance not far	43
Somebody and a nobody	44
Would you rather	45
The Art of questioning	46
A rehab so different	47
'Say My Name'	48
Without you	49
What do we crave?	50
The mystery in me	51
Never-Ending Parody	52
Be actionable	53
Doesn't feel like before	54
Nowhere at all	55
Walking alone	56
A cursed love	57
Nowhere else to seek	58
Warmth for someone	59
Wasn't raised to weep	60
Bittersweet	61
Someone who made me melt	62
Butterflies aren't gender-biased	63
Ace of spades	64
A nomad	65
Leaning on you	66
I Want You with Me	67
Accustomed to Things	68
A part of me	69
No longer in Love	70

Mind at ease	71
A better me	72
Keep your distance	73
Breakup song	74
Love is heartfelt	75
Come my way	76
Moving on without a fight	77
What I left behind	78
A walk, in time	79
Less to repent	80
Conversations	81
To a world unknown	82
A day well spent	83
When the heart bleeds	84
A Veer to the Right	85
Better than yesterday?	86
The cities inside me	87
Not A Swine	88
Feeling our own	89
Find my way home	90
A ride amongst the mountains	91
Moments to be felt	92
How you live life	93
Answers can be found	94
Mirror to your Life	95
Memories are beautiful	96
The patio from the past	97
Mother nature	98
Stopped counting days	99
One fine day	100
A morning walk	101
Tales of a Guitar	102
Lost in your smile	103
A week that went by	104
Who worked them weeds?	105
Legacy I leave behind	106
Respect for Life	107

Please do holler	108
Gather some scars	109
Let me be in harmony	110
The good things	111
A silent Goodbye	112
A sky – lovely blue	113
A Saturday night wish	114
Hide and Seek	115
Flights to catch	116
A wordless world	117
Everything's gonna be alright	118
I Love You	119
My #1 Radio station	120
Of failed love	121
Human crabs	122
What legacy?	123
Victim of my inner self	124
Pay my rent on time	125
And how	126
No date on tomorrow	127
Seek beyond	128
A stranger on the Bus	129
My naked mile	130
The city of Love	131
Maternal return	132
Think out loud	133
Behind that veil	134
To feel alive	135
Locked out thoughts	136
What am I to you?	137
On the other side	138
Irony of things	139
Walks in the park	140
A perfect adventure	142
A bloody you	143
Dreams that rust	144

Abundance of Life	145
My Bestseller	146
A doorway sky bound	147
Moving on	148
The blinking cursor	149
Beyond the mountains	150
A better place to be	151
Someone to hang on to	152
The lessons learnt	153
Someone more	154
The dung beetles	155
I too am a beast	156
The ultimate sacrifice	157
A meekly smile	158
Heart made of gold	159
Drifted too far	160
Spaces of time	161
Have a good day	162
For the younger lot	163
Kindness-Just an act away	164
Respect that Woman	165
An ode to Art and artists	166
Need, to be freed	167
A bridge of words	168
Unknown cities	169
The shaming she got	170
Leave the rest aside	171
Demons in the dark	172
A hopeful song	173
A falling leaf	174
A Late Bloomer	175
Things I have planned	176
Masterstrokes	177
Into the daylight	178
What You Once Said	180
The threads you hold	181

Story in the eyes	182
In your thoughts	183
Hey Mom, Good Morning	184
Legacies	185
An emotional hook	186
Not for fame	187
A vision unique	188
Words with shapes	189
Learned to sail	190
Into the woods	191
Nothing but Love	192
Spaces meant to hide	193
A window to the better	194
Sing along	195
Beauty called Meditation	196
Strangers called words	197
The Valentines Mug	198
Never ever	199
Till the end of time	200
Out the abyss	201
Mostly you, and us	202
Happy Women's day	204
Battle for lives	205
Bring it on	206
Save our Oceans	207
Miss you	208
A costly toss	209
A Song in my mind	210
Taken for a ride	211
Broken wings	212
Juggling life	213
Time capsule	214
Gazing in the dark	215
I tried	216
What Did I Do?	217
An unimaginable nightmare	218

Board that flight	219
Being Kind	220
Accidents	221
Technology –The boon & the doom	222
Strangers in the crowd	223
Die another day	224
Lost in your eyes	225
A place called time	226
A Thank You, not said	227
A Pizza Delivery Gone Wrong	228
The unknown, untold	229
A difference, in time	230
A bucket full of dreams	231
Something to do	232
Who painted Monday blue?	233
Humans and the brilliance	234
In Love with you	235
If I were a Bird	236
Letters not posted	237
Before my fall	238
A rainbow called Life	239
Love isn't Life	240
Daily life	241
A place named serenity	242
A probe – deeper	243
Angel from the skies	244
Remnants of our pasts	245
I called It a day	246
Some place, free	247
Unraveling Depression	248
Inside the mind of a newborn	249
A Blissful Evening	250
I Love You, Mom	252
Racism	254
The Depression Story	255

A Guitar

If I were a Guitar,

Which song would I play?

Would it be a melody?

Or rather a sarcastic parody?

Would I rigorously strum, to create tunes?

Or nonchalantly pull off ill-timed notes?

Would I inspire a soulful song?

Or fade into obscurity without a sound?

Would I even have a title, a name?

Or would I wait in line, for the so-called fame?

Would the chords I nail, make any sense,

Or would I be just another toy with strings?

Would I sound more melodious in the mountains,

Or between the sounds of bustling fountains?

Would my sounds merge with the sounds of the oceans?

Or rather fade into a cascade, then into oblivion?

My existence as a Guitar would only have a meaning,

If my master knows how to make me sing.

—*Giridhar Rajani Jaded*

Words Are All I Have

Words,
Words are all I have,
They make me feel alive,
They make me wanna fly,
They also make me cry.
Cry when the words are not mine,
Coz my words listen to me all the while.
I feel a calm like no other,
When my words don't flow, rather slither.
I feel a rush inside of me,
When I re-read most of my poetry.
If nothing else, I know what I have,
My words – the ones that make me feel alive.
We make a lovely duet, in fact a symphony,
Played out like a charm, with skill and artistry,
Taking out these words from my life,
Would put me on an infinite loop of "Who am I"?
—*Giridhar Hanumanthappa Jaded*

Inspiration: Boyzone song "Words."

A Salute to Law Enforcement

The air seems so pure in the mornings,

The sunset seems blissful to watch, in the evenings.

The parks are filled with laughter and green,

When the doors close at night, in comes a peaceful sleep.

There are plans to be made,

There's a long life to be lived,

There are life's itsy-bitsy battles to be won,

And seeds of a happy future to be sown.

There's a vacation that's coming up,

There are pictures to be taken, whilst going all on out,

There's that party to go to, on the mind,

There's a lot to do, no time to unwind,

But take a pause will you, in contemplation,

For granted do we all take our invisible freedom,

A freedom that was sought, and as well fought,

But exists as nothing more than an afterthought,

Freedom from invaders and from criminals,

Given as a gift to us by hardworking law-enforcement officials.

—*Giridhar Rachna Jaded*

Will You Be My Valentine?

Would it be scotch tonight, or wine?
Or rather waiting in a party line?
Would it be a walk in the park?
Or rather holding hands in the dark?
Would it be a drive someplace far?
Or a high-chair date in a bar?
Would it be a flight we would take?
Or rather a homely retreat?
Would it be a conversation night?
Or a faux-planned blind date?
Would it be an evening of taking vows?
Or in a theater not watching a movie, in the back rows?
Whatever be the way we celebrate tonight,
All I care to ask is '*Would you be my Valentine?*'
—*Giridhar Pavitra Jaded*

Patience

I sometimes wonder in my silent moments,
Is this all true or just a false pretense?
I sometimes wonder in thoughtful moments,
Will the end be vibrant or filled with laments?
I sometimes wonder in my blissful moments,
Why, at times, the mind wanders like gushing torrents?
I wonder and wonder until I no longer wonder,
And I find myself asking *'Should I really bother?'*
A silent breeze then rushes past my ears,
Driving some sense in and calming my fears.
A breeze of reassurance from the Universe,
Dispelled in which, beautiful horizons I shall traverse,
I crane my neck, to then listen closely, in silence,
And I hear *'All it takes sometimes is patience.'*
—*Giridhar Praful Jaded*

Love of Old Times

What was it like to love when there were no phones?
No way to connect without having to take the roads.
Was love more intense then, or is it now?
Be nice, or I shall swipe on your profile, go on now?
Was there more passion filled in lesser moments back then?
Or is it filled in spikes of today's instant gratification?
Those planned visits to the creeks and lush green mountains,
Replaced by hookups and one-night stands, and confusions?
The days and days of playing just the eye games,
Versus a fling today, breakup tomorrow, then calling names,
The days spent just planning out a surprise,
Versus moments felt at night, to be forgotten at sunrise,
If there is ever a Bible written on Love,
It has to have a lesson on how to go back, to old love.

—Giridhar Harsh Jaded

Random Thought

Real men first like to go to places inside of the minds of the women they seek,

They do not dive in blindfolded; chasing the depths between her legs.

They think.

—*Giridhar Viaan Jaded*

Random Thoughts

If all the unsaid words from everyone in the world were to be put into a box, the box would tremble, quiver, roar, and burst out more violently than a volcano. Those unspoken words want nothing more badly than making their presence felt!

—*Giridhar Krustappa Jaded*

Random Thought

There's nothing wrong with having outlandish dreams,

So long as those align with your passionate realms.

There's nothing wrong in daydreaming,

As long as it pushes you to be a better human being.

—*Giridhar Deviramma Jaded*

The Art of Meditation

There's a place I would like you to see,
It's where a lot of good is meant to be.
It's not a place too far from where you live,
As magical places appear to a mind that believes.
Where the trees are greener than a grasshopper's crown,
And the smiles are wider than you have ever known.
The mountains beckon, but it's as if hope is sown,
Into every plant, shrub, weed or tree that has grown,
There is however an acceptance only for the humankind,
As dreams fly free, and there's time to unwind.
This place isn't anywhere but inside your mind,
It's a place you spend most of your life.
Why not pick up a broom and start to clean?
Practice an art, or head for that run under the sun,
Learn to tame your thoughts, or plainly learn meditation.
And once you do, this place I wanted to show you,
Would have already become a part of you;
—*Giridhar Kashibai Jaded*

Something about you

I just can't stop loving you,
Having known who's, the real you.
I have seen your blushes,
I have known your wishes,
I have adored your tresses,
I felt myself in your kisses.
I can't stop thinking about you,
Have given up fighting those thoughts now.
I have lived your decisions,
Experienced your confusions,
Reasoned without any reasons,
I felt myself grow through your delusions.
I can't stop being with you,
Having learned that it takes two to tango,
I have seen you shy as well as cry,
Skipped a heartbeat when you jumped in joy.

—*Giridhar Manohar Jaded*

The bygone winter

It's that time of the year again,

When we look surprised at the sight of rains,

It's around this time, we walked the frozen streets,

Wearing the thick sweaters and matching wind cheats,

We walked around with giggles, and grinning from ear to ear,

Wouldn't take much back then, for a smile to appear.

Those leather jackets that we wore all day,

With words *'Live to Love another day'*,

Just to five words had an ocean of emotions to convey,

We were oblivious to what the world had to say.

The million perfumes which we tried at the mall,

Careless and lost in our aura, whilst only love stood tall.

I sometimes wonder if evil eyes exist,

Nothing else can explain our dramatic twist.

Aliens like silence, anger, avoidance, and false pretense,

Have made their way between us, and this absolutely makes no sense.

—*Giridhar Padma Jaded*

Memories worth making

I have been after something,
Chasing that pristine smile of yours.
I have been often hallucinating,
Dreaming about our unlived years.
I have been eternally waiting,
For that perfect moment to make 'Me,' 'Us.'
I have been half living,
Saving a half for when I give you a ring.
I have noticed your shy smile,
I have noticed your mischievous guile,
I have noticed your every little gesture,
I have felt thrills from our-to be-adventures.
Time, they say is a great healer,
I say, it's also a pesky tormentor.
Come along now, I am tired waiting,
I want those memories worth making.

—*Giridhar Linganagouda Jaded*

A distant country

Every time that you come close to me,
I can sense my breath getting heavy.
Every time that you kiss me,
I feel a little spark inside of me.
Every time that you touch me,
I feel a new part inside of me.
Every time you make me laugh,
I become numb to any and every strife.
Every time you call my name,
I feel an acceptance, all over again,
Every time that we make love,
I feel frozen, like a scarecrow,
But every time that you hurt me,
I feel like running away, to a distant country.
—*Giridhar Geeta Jaded*

The demons inside me

Dark clouds hovering above my head, up high,
Even as the world sees a clear blue sky.
There's sunshine out there for the world so wide,
Yet slouched in darkness - why is it that I hide?
What are these demons inside of me?
That keep me from uniting with my destiny.
They take me to places I never want to be,
If you ask me, its not a good place to be.
But if the demon has the force, I too am in a way, fierce,
Your talent in inducing tears, my way of battling fears,
Your lure of darkness versus my thread of hope,
Your slimy touch versus my intent filled gropes,
I wasn't taught to sit aside on a ride,
With my throttle beneath my feet, I would rather drive.
Bring on your best, for I ain't going down so light,
Only a few scars I see on you, time to set that right!
—*Giridhar Vijayalakshmi Jaded*

My renaissance song

Words are all I have with me now,
As my actions from the past, weak and shallow,
Falling into an abyss I was, all this while,
You pulled me from the depths, made me worthwhile,
I was scared, I was insanely lost,
But I ain't letting my dreams sit, and rot,
I have been mad, I have been angry,
At times clinging onto ropes of insanity.
If you think I have been strong,
You have been my renaissance song.
You are the reason I am alive,
I was choking – then given a new lease of life.
I have shown you the worst, caused you unrest,
Now it's time for you to open your eyes to only the best.

—Giridhar Ashok Jaded

Have a joyful ride

I wonder at what point in one's life,
Does a child really come alive?
To an awareness which is hard to belie,
One to live knowing, for the rest of their lives.
For the world until that point in time,
Was a freebie parade, and a crisscross of lines?
For everyone around was being a good human,
Caring and loving, being ladies and gentlemen.
But then a realization, it slowly dawns,
Starts to separate the knights from the pawns,
With cracks now seen, out in the open,
From eyes that were sleeping, having finally opened,
To an existence of a societal divide,
Amidst the masses, and the things they hide,
And for a child with nothing but dream filled eyes,
It seems like an animated show, of deceits and lies,
To listen to a heart or be worked up by bitcoins?
Where did we mess up in designing this slide?
It has green, yellow but slimy - quite a joyful ride?

—*Giridhar Ramanagouda Jaded*

A little more alive

A visit to a museum is usually frowned upon,
For those silent walks do seem long and drawn,
Reveling in history isn't like a sing along,
For some stories have a gloomy face, forlorn,
Whilst there are others, who hold their own,
In a carnival of greatness, most without the crowns,
For when the bones become one, with Mother Earth,
There isn't a tremor, an eruption or a thud,
What's left though, are stories written line after line,
By the ones who saw more than the usual kind,
To see shining human might, in the walks of life,
Stories that hide, and those with an encapsulating vibe.
For as long as the human spirit erupts and shines,
There will be writers to pen down them vines.
And even for a moment, in standing on one's feet, feeling raw,
The heart it transforms, like the Great Yellowstone Thaw,
For the way we are, in flesh and brimming with life,
They lived and died too but were a little more alive.

—*Giridhar Anysuya Jaded*

Blinking eyes

Aren't all of us lonely in some little way,
Feeling whole a while, then losing our way,
For life's short but rather long as well,
Tossing twists, riveting turns it dispels,
And in those moments spent being whole,
Lies a hypnotic sword that pierces a hole,
Filling that void, is a newfound vigorous role,
Not knowing it's the beginning of a mole,
That could grow and engulf a lively soul,
By dispelling it into the loneliness abode,
Where darkness lurks at every single blink,
And the feelings run amok, up till that ugly brink,
Where everyone's an enemy including oneself,
Those moments in life are best left, unfelt,
Whilst out on a patrol out there, I see many a blinking eye,
Each waiting a turn, to fight and get back to the light.
—*Giridhar Subhash Jaded*

Lost in Your Brown Hues

How do I describe your eyes?
When all I muster to do, is to get lost?
Like a toddler fiddling with a train of thought,
Like a teenager wrestling with crushes and skin-pops,
Trying hard to gather my line of thought,
But no matter how hard I try, I just cannot.
I see the beauty in them, and I see hope in them,
I see that it works better, when in tandem,
I fail to notice the lines, by your eyeballs,
For its in your brown hue does reside, my pitfall,
I won't say sorry about not being able to depict your eyes,
As being lost in them at times, feels worthwhile.

—*Giridhar Myna Jaded*

Gratitude filled kiss

The fish delectably served on your plate,
Is from an ocean or a clear water lake.
While you treat your taste buds, do you ever wonder,
How did it end up on your platter?
A fisherman or two went into the wild,
Not jungles but the wilderness of the tides,
And they play with their sleep and even their lives,
To come home empty-handed at times, or with crates full of fish.
Some of them were vegan, yet set out on the sail,
For they had mouths to feed, couldn't afford to fail,
They sail for days and months sometimes,
Being missed and missing family at the same time.
The next time you are about to eat your fish,
Don't forget to send a fisherman a gratitude-filled kiss.

—Giridhar Vasundhara Jaded

2:00 AM thoughts

It's 2:00 a.m., and I lay wide awake,
Sheer darkness in the absence of light.
It's warm inside, and my bed feels alright,
Then I start to sense a chill down my spine.
I curl up under the sheets; but it doesn't help.
I shudder to think about crying out for help.
I see myself curled up in a corner outside,
No sign of my blanket, and a pitch black presides.
There comes the wolf - drooling by its jaws.
Looks menacing with those eyes and shiny claws,
It makes a sadistic moan as it hears the footsteps,
Of its approaching master – a demon named loneliness.
I lay there motionless and sense-struck,
Shivering, trying to think, what do I do next.
—*Giridhar Shrikant Jaded*

The Poetry in You

There's poetry in the way you look at me,
There's poetry in the way you smile at me,
There's poetry in the way you make me smile,
There's poetry in the way you make me wanna fly.
You make me feel what money can't buy,
So why do I sometimes, end up feeling dry?
Is there poetry in the way you lie?
Is there poetry in leaving me high and dry?
Only to come back when you need an alibi,
Treating me like a motel - worse than an outcast who didn't even try,
There's poetry in the way you delectably hide,
There's poetry in the way you seamlessly glide,
Into the masses following the latest ride,
And seeing you go, I am glad I stand on this side.

—Giridhar Pavan Jaded

Smiles Are Free

Smile all you can,

For the smiles are free.

Care all you can,

For compassion is free.

Listen to yourself,

For those thoughts are free.

Work all you can,

That passion, too, is free.

Travel all you can,

The world's your oyster to be.

Love all you can,

For hate is an avoidable anomaly,

Live life the best way you can, be a little giddy,

Time won't wait; it isn't your best buddy.

—Giridhar Apoorva Jaded

You by my side

You left me alone when I wasn't ready,

My armpits were sweaty, hands far from steady.

You left me alone when I wasn't well,

My emotions grew into beasts, summoned from the depths of hell.

You left me alone when I needed you the most,

My directions were haywire - I was clearly lost.

You left me when you should have been by my side,

It's alright darling - I now have a full throttle on my ride,

And in doing so, you helped me choose my side,

Where at least I am in the clear, and I shall glide,

And I am glad to not have you by my side.

—Giridhar Prashanth Jaded

The Birds in Words

Aren't words a type of birds?
For they flap across oceans, to then be heard?
They can even fly over the mountains,
They can pierce the wind or the canyons,
Words can emanate from one soul,
To then be known by another, to then be whole,
And make someone feel alive, again,
Yet remain as words, with nothing to be gained.
Words are like messengers,
And can also become avengers,
Words can carry compassion,
And as well can transform slumber into action,
Words written or spoken can be those wings,
That transform simple things into beautiful things,
Words are way more influencing,
Than what we are conditioned into believing.
—*Giridhar Madhura Jaded*

Say No to wasting food

The food that you stow away,
Only to be later thrown away,
Or the food that you leave behind,
While at an exquisite restaurant,
Or the extra snacks that you elegantly stow,
Until smelly, and finally out the window,
All that food is yours by right,
And you have earned it, even put on a fight,
But everything we do is connected by a chain, invisible to plain sight.
A simple thought accepted by the masses as an act,
Can transform lives in millions and that's a fact.
Take for instance the plastic straw revolution,
We at least have a lower number, now in circulation,
Eliminate your food waste and the distribution shall alter,
Reaching more to where there's a need or hunger.
You will feel lighter and a part of a cause,
If nothing else, you got more bucks in your purse.

—Giridhar Mridula Jaded

People that matter

Words sometimes said are not meant to be,
The way they really turned out to be.
Not every mistake is an unforgivable sin,
Forgive friends, family, your kith and kin.
The heart grows bigger when you forgive,
Grudges can die, but you are meant to live.
Loneliness and despair can make us erupt,
Forgiveness, compassion will make it melt.
If nothing else, you are making someone feel better,
What's life without a few people that matter!

—Giridhar Kiran Jaded

To Love or Be Loved?

Is it easier to be loved?
Or to plainly love?
Both need a pinch of Art,
To really light up a spark,
Not through fake smiles,
Not through unending lies,
Not through misguided affection,
Not through an instant attraction,
Not from pressure, or from stress,
Not from an inner greed to impress,
But with feelings that revel in abysmal depths,
And with actions bereft of expectations.
Be in love or admire it from far - there's no in-between,
—*Giridhar Tejraj Jaded*

A careless world

Souls colder than ice,
Insecurity driving a game of cats and mice,
Not many to care for the deaf, dumb, or the mute.
Emotions toyed around, smile and being rude,
Turning a blind eye to them weeping souls,
And walk in false pride, like them ghouls,
Being frozen in the heart is honestly a façade,
For even the coldest of heart is soft, that's how it was made,
Self-gains driving most of the upper cream,
Not knowing their decisions can make or break them dreams,
Walking the Earth being blind to possibilities that love brings,
Some live lives not knowing how to live.
And living a life not knowing how to give,
Is that really even a way to live?

—*Giridhar Naveen Jaded*

A winter morning run

The winter chill swept through my spine,
As I stepped out, determined to walk a mile.
The freshness in the air was overshadowed,
By the rising discomfort in my back, from cold,
I shrugged it off and went along,
A few yards later, my mind started humming a song.
A melodious slumber calling me back to bed,
I looked back once and walked ahead as fast as I could tread,
For in that moment I looked back, there was a chemistry,
Between a sleepy me and its ally named lethargy,
And even though I love being witness to their love story,
I have no intention of seeing their prospering family,
I am selfish that way, I walk on anyways,
Knowing it's alright I shall make it even, my own way,
These moments of restraint last barely a few seconds,
Once overcome often, might be looked upon as well mastered errands.

—*Giridhar Nitin Jaded*

Take good care of your life

If you have had a heart attack,
It probably was a necessary whack.
Like they say it's never too late,
Caring for yourself is your decision to make.
Life's nothing but 24 hours given day after day,
Why not hustle a little more, keep moving anyway?
A few more steps every day is a deal,
You need to make to help yourself heal.
A few cautious bites every day,
Soon enough your heart shall sing and maybe even sway,
A few hours working out breaking a sweat,
Shall help you get back on your feet.
What if you haven't had a heart attack?
Don't wait for one - just take care, don't be waiting for a smack.

—*Giridhar Nandan Jaded*

Trolling

Trolling is an obsession,

Maybe a dear sibling of depression,

It emanates out of frustration,

A cautious act of attracting attention.

What joy if any in body shaming?

What pleasure if any is there in trolling?

But if trolling makes you feel better,

All I got for you is my MIDDLE FINGER!

—*Giridhar Deepthi Jaded*

Note: Poetry can emanate out of anger too. This one came out when someone started off calling my poetry as mediocre and kept going a level up, caught up in a downward literary diarrhea.

Love Your Demeanor

I like it when your lips quiver,

I like it when goosebumps make you shiver,

I like it when your lips flutter,

I like your bear hugs and everything thereafter.

I like everything about your demeanor,

Except when lies make your lips quiver, and your words stutter.

—Giridhar Abhishek Jaded

Healthy Living

The air smells quite thin and pure,
Everyone out here is looking for a cure.
There's the disinfectant smell in the air,
Coupled with the smell of a hand sanitizer.
There are smiling faces and gloomy faces,
The body has hit back; it rebels leaving behind traces.
Some are hopeful, some are joyous,
Some look lost while some are anxious.
A newborn here, a soul departed there,
All facets of life, they are all out here,
Some are here naturally, while others were forced to be.
Healthy living isn't a chore but a lifestyle, a necessity,
I would choose the latter amidst a Hospital and Hospitality.
—*Giridhar Shwetha Jaded*

TGIF

Thank God It's Friday,

For a Friday's always a good day,

As it rides alongside a Saturday and Sunday.

But is it really a TGIF feeling every Friday?

Or is the wannabe in you wanting to make hay,

For there a lot to show and tell in the world today,

How many things we do on those weekends?

Are nothing more than a means to an end?

A weekend can also be spent unwinding,

From a week at work and just spent plainly living,

And when it comes to the things worth doing,

To go all in for that's when it's worth remembering,

A life lived isn't depicted by the count of things we do,

Rather from moments lived feeling them all the way through,

Have a great weekend!

—*Giridhar Avinash Jaded*

Moments of pure bliss

The world is a canvas for an artist,
To find newer ways to sprinkle their own mist,
Some use colors, some use sketches,
Some use the sounds, some make Art digging trenches,
Some rely solely on their voice,
Some paint as words bringing their imagination to life,
Through words that cause an emotional renaissance.
Whilst some use sand, or make Art out of ice,
Some use their persona, while some find their calling in a grain of rice.
It's a belief about being unique that makes an Artist who he or she is,
Living life in turmoil more, but also dispelling in moments of pure bliss.

—Giridhar Pratik Jaded

Just let it be

What is love to you isn't love to me,

Dare you compare an opera to a clumsy lullaby,

What is affection to you isn't affection to me,

Dare you compare an accidental penny drop with philanthropy,

What is right for you isn't right for me,

Dare you compare a minuscule event in the
past to a whimsical future to be.

What I am to you is not what you are to me,

So, let's just not argue any further and just let it be!

—Giridhar Karthik Jaded

Art Rocks

There is art in the way you can walk,
There is art in the way you can talk.
There is art in the way you can cook,
There is art in the way you read a book.
There is art in the way you live,
There is art in the way you can give.
There is art in the way you think,
So too is there art in the way you wink.
The greatest art of all though,
Is art on a path less followed,
The path taken by an artist unknown,
To experience, imagine, and then to unfold,
Those thoughts no matter how fresh or outgrown,
Lay bare in an inner self, to wither or be known.
Art ROCKS!
—*Giridhar Rashmi Jaded*

Continue Being in Love

What makes me come back to you?
What makes me yearn for you?
Pertinent questions I intend to see through.
For answers, the only way to wade through,
But sometimes I wonder why,
For I do not believe my feelings to be naive,
In halfhearted answers, can one really hide?
Maybe one day those locks shall be withdrawn,
And we shall sing our own melodious love song,
Or maybe there is a peace in not knowing,
In just being and to continue loving.

—*Giridhar Preethi Jaded*

A chance not far

In moments where you feel you are plunging into an abyss,
Find that something worthy of being missed,
Something that pulls you back a couple of feet outwards,
Even if for a brief second, making you feel you could take on the sword,
And swing it over the ropes pulling you down,
Each representing a problem you have made your own,
For the difference between someone who gave up,
And someone who decided to fight, to not hang up,
Is that fleeting moment that got you nowhere,
Yet placed you on a pedestal to getting somewhere.

—*Giridhar Amit Jaded*

Somebody and a nobody

Every day that you step out for a run or a walk is a victory.
No one can deny that it isn't a tad bit easy.
Your mind's the devil to conquer, well before your body,
That's the difference between a fit somebody and a lethargic wannabe.
There's a bliss in positivity emanating from physical activities,
At times from taking, other times sharing it
with others becomes your destiny!

—Giridhar Deepak Jaded

Would you rather

Would you rather suffer from lack of sleep due to wanting to be awake?
Then from depression, and whatever it holds at stake,
Would you rather fight the world for what is right?
Then being engulfed in suffocation, from its vice,
Would you rather speak out your mind and come out on a clean slate?
Then living in confusion, and giving in to envy, greed or hate.

—*Giridhar Prashanth Jaded*

The Art of questioning

Did I wind up where I am today?

Or did I crawl along a crowded pathway?

Do I stand here knowing myself better?

Or did I gather more questions than answers?

Do I look in the mirror now and smile?

Or do I carry a condescending grin, dry & wry?

Questioning in life is better than answering,

There's some tantalizing fun in searching, in knowing and just being.

—*Giridhar Krishna Jaded*

A rehab so different

The skies look beautiful and an effervescent blue,
The trees are dressed in green – looking new,
The winds are mild as if trying to be gentle,
It certainly feels peaceful in nature's ensemble.
A long breath that goes inside,
When I am at peace, with nature by my side,
Does take away bruises from what's called life,
Everyone needs a rehab, and nature is mine.

—Giridhar Sudha Jaded

'Say My Name'

C'mon, 'Say my name,' he said,
And she did, gathering as much gumption as she held,
Emotions erupted sky high in the nightly air,
He felt elated hearing his name called out loud and clear.
It's been a month, and she hasn't called his name.
Hence the 'Say my name.'
She did, and smiled as she had a moment of remembrance.
Forever forgetful, she suffered from Alzheimer's!

—Giridhar Shobha Jaded

Without you

What would I do without you,
Oh, my beautiful mind?
How would I write down?
The unwritten - one of its kind?
A wholesome lot, is what you put me through,
But by now I am used to your grind,
All I asked is to be well guided,
To do the right things right and do so being kind.
Thoughts, they simmer in me all the while,
It's tiring, but pluck as many as I can, walking my mile.

—*Giridhar Shilpa Jaded*

What do we crave?

An unexpected conversation,
A kindness filled action,
An unexpected hug,
To be smitten by the love-bug,
An unexpected victory,
A heart filled with empathy,
Isn't that all we crave at times?
It doesn't take a lot to spread smiles.
—*Giridhar Kittu (Pramod) Jaded*

The mystery in me

What makes me 'me' is a mystery,
That I wish to unfold one day, in sanctity,
I like the confusions as well, that reside,
Amidst the vibes that help me to glide,
Being sorted is akin to imprisonment to me,
Battling it out to learn, rather my trajectory,
My thoughts are who I am,
My confusions, they take me closer to who I am.

—Giridhar Sunil Jaded

Never-Ending Parody

What is love?

Tell me if you will.

Is it a soulful chorus or a dreary lullaby?

What is compassion?

Tell me if you will.

Is it an abundant ocean or a toxic puddle in obscurity?

What is purpose?

Tell me if you will.

Is it something set it stones or quivers like an anomaly?

Who am I?

Tell me if you will.

I am a nobody, trying to grab the central vein of destiny.

—*Giridhar Mamatha Jaded*

Be actionable

The number of sleepless nights you have,
Do not define you as a person at all,
It's the moments you spend wide awake,
And in between, the actions that you take,
That define how many peaceful nights you shall have,
Where you are yourself, sleeping with a gentle smile.
Be actionable.
—*Giridhar Suresh Jaded*

Doesn't feel like before

We don't talk our hearts out anymore,
It certainly doesn't feel like before.
To give up is not something I learned.
To fill it all up, something I never yearned,
To give in to reasons that don't matter,
Is like a ripple in isolated waters,
For it occurs merely as an incident then,
With no bearing on what needs to be done.
What I can fix though, is all in my hands,
There's no respite from life and its errands.

—Giridhar Shashan Jaded

Nowhere at all

I moved through silent waters,
Until cold didn't affect me at all.
I moved through the lives of hordes of people,
Until I realized I hadn't come far after all.
I moved through a whirlwind of envy,
Until I stopped feeling envy at all,
I have watched the cleaner souls get corrupted,
I've been witness to when raw human emotions erupted,
In retrospect, I wonder where is it that I have reached?
Have I come far ahead or reached nowhere at all?

—*Giridhar Sunil Jaded*

Walking alone

I was walking alone,
Until I found someone,
Who gave me warmth at first,
But then left me out in the cold,
Now I know that I was better off on my own
Minus the scars, whilst I was walking alone!
—*Giridhar Sharath Jaded*

A cursed love

A warming smile and a welcoming face;
Abrupt laughter, and a conversation shared;
About earnest dreams and endless hopes,
A youthful camaraderie, it engulfs them both.
The light from their faces, it warms our heart,
Until those dark secrets find their way on out.
Yet the beacon shines on, with never ending care;
For in matters of love, everything seemed fair.
Their laughter never ceased,
The conversations went on without any ends,
Books, movies, music, and forever it went,
A few worries were dispelled, to be banished, sent.
An uplifting word, when one felt dejected,
A helping hand, when the other felt rejected;
A warm hug, to fight away those fears,
As fondness grew, in came the envious, with spears,
The past came calling, two hearts started to waiver,
The longing in their eyes turns into a cold, persistent fear,
One stood strong, while the other surrendered,
Unable to make sense, quivered and eventually faltered,
Call it a cursed bond or inescapable fate,
Their abode of happiness was brought down by hate,

—*Giridhar Rakesh Jaded*

Nowhere else to seek

Hearts that bleed have little or no greed,
And hearts with a demonic ego to feed,
Tears shed from moments of compassion,
Soul hardened to all forms of emotions,
Hardened only on the outside though,
Boiling inside they form carbon walls.
Bleed and burn until they're pitch dark,
Until finally, there's nowhere else to park.
A smile here, a teardrop there,
Sometimes there isn't a lot left, for some to care,
And is only fair so long as we can breathe the air,
To be kind to one another, with a green cloak of humanity to wear,
Find an ailing heart and pass along a needed hug,
For some never learned to ask, to tug.

—Giridhar Praveen Jaded

Warmth for someone

Your uncomfortable chill down the spine,

Can be a moment of freedom for someone.

Your moment of utter confusion,

Can be certain, imminent, death for someone.

Your moment of work anxiety,

Can be an irreversible breakup for someone.

Your moment of a sleepless night,

Can be an inhumane craving of warmth for someone.

Every time a worry engulfs your mind,

Remember there's someone who would die
to swap, leaving their all behind.

—*Giridhar Vishal Jaded*

Wasn't raised to weep

Under these treacherous mountains,
Beneath these hideous seasons,
Under the burning rays of the sun,
Beneath dark clouds, that never seem to move on,
I stand here and stare at the Sun, head on.
My eyes are weary, but not by choice.
But I ain't someone to be caught up in a vice,
I look around for a spark somewhere,
But all I see are signs that not many cares,
For life's a parade of unending wants,
From the depths of desires to material wants,
A parade good enough to be called a carnival,
To then be left stranded as a lonesome cardinal,
I trod along - now a master at ignoring,
Knowing well that in sleepless nights, there is no mooring.
The weary eyes are gifts from a lack of sleep,
As the fire in me, it runs miles down deep,
And my Dad and Mom, they didn't raise me to weep,
Wanted me to be one who could make promises to keep,
If life's a bitch, I'm a black magic witch,
I am here and will keep churning my tricks.

—*Giridhar Ravi Jaded*

A nomad

I am a nomad in my own world,
Hanging onto life by a double-edged sword.
I am a traveler in my own spaces,
Sorting memories from those sacred places.
I am a visitor in my own realm,
Walking in naked, and without a veil,
I am a tormentor in my own mind,
Raising questions gentle, as well as wild.
I am a solicitor in my own shop,
I like to choose, not to aimlessly hop.
I am a janitor of my own mess,
I wipe my heart too, not just my flesh.
I am hard-working in my own ways,
Doing it right, not just because it pays.
I am a lot, yet I am very less,
Just don't have time for the unwanted stress.
—*Giridhar Vinayak Jaded*

Leaning on you

Under the glow of silver moonlight,
Would you just hold on to me tight?
My heart is heavy, I had a fight,
Would you make me feel alright?
I am not shy, for I come running to you,
Only you make me wanna see this through,
Under the rays of the sun shining bright,
Would you just hold on to me tight?
My mind is racing, these worries make me weak,
Some solace in your arms is all I seek,
I am not scared, but I seek refuge in you,
With you by my side, fear seems an alien hue.
Would you make me sleep, I wanna be with you?
If leaning on you is love too, yeah – I Love you.

—Giridhar Ramakrishna Jaded

I Want You with Me

When the sun goes down,
When the moon comes up,
When the stars fall down,
When the night goes long,
I want you with me.

If the lights go out,
If life hits me hard,
If my sail gets rough,
If the days seem long,
I want you with me.

When my smiles are back,
When my wings do flap,
When I soar into the sky,
When I set things right,
I want you with me.

—*Giridhar Daniel Jaded*

Accustomed to Things

Mind - accustomed to confusions,
Body - accustomed to diseases,
Soul - accustomed to separations,
Heart - accustomed to delusions,
Life - accustomed to disruptions,
Love - accustomed to illusions,
Faith - accustomed to interrogations,
Hope - accustomed to fearful demons,
Smiles - accustomed to deceptions,
Purpose - accustomed to compulsions,
Compassion - accustomed to intentions,
Reasons - are they even reasons now, or rather fiction imaginations?
—*Giridhar Vikas Jaded*

Mind at ease

Sometimes I feel like running out,
To get up and just be out there,
For the possibilities seem endless,
Mesmerizing, the lure of the world beckons,
With a tantalizing tease hard to match,
Egging me on to go find my catch,
The window curtains grin at me,
The gas in my car mocks at me,
I shudder, amazed by its power,
At how feeble the human mind is – Oh, dear.
Wanting is an agony aunt in disguise,
Whose presence I truly and utterly despise.
I open a notepad, and I start to type,
Agony aunt took a flight; and my mind is now at ease.
—*Giridhar Amruth Jaded*

A better me

I walk these empty streets,
I wake up to fresh linen sheets,
I lay awake some long nights,
Often times lost in thought.

I hear these unknown voices,
Which come and go leaving feeble traces,
I let them fill this tranquil silence,
Often feeling overwhelmed, in every sense.

I see these unknown shadows,
Which touch my innermost shallows,
I let them get in and come out,
Often creating a poem or a song.

I drift into unknown spaces,
Listen to, and see their gentle faces,
I let them be kind to me,
For they make me a better me.
—*Giridhar Vinit Jaded*

A walk, in time

It was a sunny and blissful dawn,
Tied my shoelaces, stepped onto my lawn,
Warmed up for the day and headed on out,
Said hello to the yellow pond fish with a pout.
Jogged outside, came across the road of envy,
I walked along in search of another alley.
Kept walking, came across the road of hatred,
Felt fumes on my body, took the next left.
Went ahead, came across misery avenue,
Ran from there, wanted something new.
Miles ahead saw a glittering sign of greed,
Fought my way out despite being pulled.
Hobbling on, I saw the road of violence,
Closed my eyes and walked in silence.
I then felt an aura stepping onto the next path,
It was the road of kindness that I walked with a happy heart.

—*Giridhar Venugopal Jaded*

Less to repent

I will build you a castle if you like,
With walls of conviction from reinforced tiles,
And sprinkle my affection on the inside,
To act like gems that glisten in the sunlight,
I will furnish it by wisdom at every corner,
To banish all worries least they try to enter,
I will lay a carpet laced with heartfelt feelings,
With an aroma not found in the worldly things.
I will drape them curtains made of chivalry,
To respect you the way every girl needs to be,
I will add quotes on walls with my life's lessons,
To act as a guiding light in those darker moments,
I will fill the air with care and love to no end,
To make the place a home, with very less to repent.

—*Giridhar Shivanand Jaded*

A day well spent

A day well spent in my books,
Is when I have been good,
Or when I have been told I have been kind,
Or if a little gesture of mine evoked a smile,
From a dear one, or from an absolute stranger,
Or an act of courage on something that mattered,
Something that made my heart swell with pride,
Something that made the day a worthwhile ride,
Or when I venture out into mother nature,
Feel the cold, the sun, the wind, and the weather,
Or when a far-off tear gets held back, through my words,
Or my words helped someone be inspired, feel a little bold,
Or when a deed long back, that I might have done,
Came in return as not much but a smile outgrown,
Or when my thoughts flow like silent water,
At first, but then end up creating a poem and a flutter.
—*Giridhar Karthik Jaded*

When the heart bleeds

When the heart bleeds, there's no sound,
It seeps inside slowly and goes on around,
In swirls that wrench the gut from inside,
Toss and turn all you will, it just won't subside.
The dark clouds make it hard to see,
A blessing in disguise though, is not seeing oneself bleed.

When the heart bleeds, there's no sound,
Doesn't matter how often the sun goes down,
The time of the day ceases to exist,
Sadistic thoughts are impossible to resist.
A feeling of being lost, even in a crowded place,
Loiters around looking for a moment of solace.

When the heart bleeds, there's certainly a choice,
To let it bleed or to find a way out of its vice.
—Giridhar Pramod Jaded

The cities inside me

I sometimes believe that inside me,
Reside a few cities seen and unseen,
They call on my name from time to time,
In hushed whispers that are obviously not mine,
I feel drawn into an otherworldly spell,
For good or worse, only time shall tell,
Blindingly encapsulating is the unknown,
Out of the window, the frivolous fears are long gone.
I now experience a certain bliss in traveling,
As I silently watch the growth in my own being,
Strangers' faces, and random acts of kindness,
Or even haywire plans, and foolish decisions,
Beautiful places, a near empty tank of gas,
Life doesn't, but these experiences certainly last.
I like it when the cities call out my name,
Keeping me the same, yet not keeping me the same,

—*Giridhar Vijay Jaded*

Not A Swine

I don't know if she smiles at me,
But I sense it, as she comes running to me,
I feel loved when she latches onto me,
Didn't know this space resided in me,
Every day I feel the same warmth,
Even when I am down or just playing my part,
She loves me unconditionally, and it's true,
She even wants to follow me into the loo,
She's not afraid of catching my cold,
Doesn't say much, not much left untold,
The best part is making me feel that I belong,
Want her by my right, never by my wrong,
I am proud of the day I had made her mine,
She's my pup, my love, dare you call her a swine.

—*Giridhar Adarsh Jaded*

Feeling our own

Let's go someplace, kick some rocks,
Getting rid of the shoes and them socks,
Let's go someplace, nice and quiet,
Sharing our vibes, making it light,
Let's go someplace, shiny and bright,
Hang our coats, bask in the twilight,
Let's go someplace, far yet near,
From prying eyes that prick, O' dear,
Let's go someplace, have some fun,
Be ourselves, answerable to none,
Let's go someplace, eat some pops,
Have a night where no one is counting shots,
Let's go someplace, make some love,
Baskin' in one another's presence, c'mon now,
Let's go someplace, serene and calm,
Where you can be you, and I feel my own.
—*Giridhar Rajani Jaded*

Find my way home

I sometimes walk into empty spaces,
Feeling lost and drawn, around those crevices,
I see shapes that seem like faces,
Or scars from my past as ugly patches.
I wash them up, I soap them dry,
Not seeing them go, my heart fantasizes a measly cry,
They stir me up, they make me vulnerable,
No one taught them to be gentle or feeble.
It doesn't pain like real physical pain,
Making me wonder what's the real gain,
Lost in these spaces, I grope for light,
Gasping for air, looking for my way out, treading light,
And then I see that little glimmer of hope,
Laced in white feathers, it lends me a rope,
I grab it hard and find my way home,
Content that I won't have to go back into that gloom.
—*Giridhar Hanumanthappa Jaded*

A ride amongst the mountains

Overlooking the mountains, the ride was rather nice,
As snow covered trails passed by the side,
The breath in my lungs felt really alright,
Was I breathing before? I thought I'd nailed it right,
A kid in the bus pulled another's cap and laughed,
In came a poke, on the back of his head,
On another seat a duo shared silence,
Not by choice but due to uncalled for indifference,
In the corner though, I saw a spark,
A first date seemed to light up their dark,
An elderly woman sat, and she people watched,
Reminiscing over memories, lost in her past,
A youngster listened to his music all the while,
Counting steps to his dreams, trying hard to hide his smile,
I let my thoughts fly, and my eyes go dry,
There's peace in thoughts and places we seldom try.

—*Giridhar Rachna Jaded*

Moments to be felt

Green blades of grass on the ground,
Dewdrops that glistened and looked round,
It was the wind that caused the tremble,
Hanging tight was the grass, despite the wobbles,
The sunlight kissed my skin, spreading some warmth,
As a relief filled sigh escaped my breath,
My thoughts narrowed, and made a thin line,
They listen to me most of the time,
I felt myself shrink and my body relax,
The present feeling overwhelmed over life's hard facts.
I basked in the moment, but was a little scared,
To lose this trance and such moments that I care,
Moments like these are meant to be felt,
At times, the mind needs a hiatus from the unrest.

—*Giridhar Pavitra Jaded*

How you live life

A painting on the wall sees it all,
The smiles, the cries, even someone's fall.
From piling up dishes in the kitchen sink,
To someone being pushed to the brink.
From the settling dust in corners and walls,
To a pile of shopping bags from the mall,

A painting on the wall sees it all,
The laughs, the moans, and love standing tall,
From crazy parties to silent talks,
To spontaneous plans and morning walks.
From harmless banter to full-blown fights,
To constant chatter and the Christmas lights.

A painting on the wall sees it all,
Spilled coffee, emotions, and widening walls,
What that painting sees, is in your hands,
It's how you live, there's not really any magic wand.

—Giridhar Praful Jaded

Answers can be found

Moments that define us are by and far,
Carving out the dreams is what defines who we are,
Moments of indecision, indeed a slimy demon,
Defining the threads that you shall then summon.
In such moments, take a few deep breaths, or head out for a walk,
Ain't any way better to clear your thoughts.
Talk it out, seek your advice all around,
Think in solace, for then the answers can be found.
A failure here, a sweet victory there,
Keep marching though, and the outcome shall be fair.
If not fair, at least you know deep inside,
Towards your dreams, you started your slide,
If it's easy, it probably isn't meant to be,
Intoxicating is every step to your destiny.
Pull up those socks and head on out now,
Dreams remain distant if all your head does, is rest on a pillow.
—*Giridhar Harsh Jaded*

Mirror to your Life

The mirror is your BFF of all,
Baring the truth even when you bare it all.
The sleep filled eyes, the poignant looks, it sees it all,
Witnesses a success or a crashing fall.
A morning wink, a gaiety dance,
Or an anguish filled face, or that hopeful glance.
Even the stories from decades gone by, it sees it all,
Between you two, can there ever be a wall?
From wary eyes to dream drunk eyes,
To affectionate hugs, and eyes with questions that pry,
A mirror creates a mystique world of its own,
Showing you the true you, a love affair unknown.
A hoarse song, or that practiced frown,
It's a space where a million thoughtful seeds are sown,
Try loving yourself more and the one you see in your mirror,
Do that which makes your smile grow naturally wider.

—Giridhar Viaan Jaded

Note: BFF implies Best Friend Forever.

Memories are beautiful

The river's edge bridge at Lewisville,
Overlooking the beautiful canyon lake,
Where we watched many a sunset;
Even in winter, whilst tucked inside a blanket,
I remember the silence of the glistening waters,
And the one-off fish, jumping out to check on air.
Do you remember the shapely rock pile?
The one we built meticulously besides a street sign.
Your hands, soft and cold as always,
Me, rubbing them and into the lake, dropping my shades.
I don't cry over the lost shades now,
Maybe I do, over the less frequent visits though.
I have that picture from back then in my wallet,
Where you posed, my lovely, with a blue pellet.
It's a little worn now but lives safely on my phone.
It's just a still but those movements, moments
are in my mind, on their own.

—*Giridhar Krustappa Jaded*

The patio from the past

The apartment patio overlooking the pool,
Where we timelessly sat on footstools,
With an extra cushion for your tender buns.
Holding hands, watching those rains,
We don't live there anymore, the place though resides in me,
As a faint little satin thread in my gigantic memory.
We failed miserably trying to get a squirrel,
To share our patio, even for a little while.
I even remember some of those talks,
Even the words, lines, and your expressions and laughing gags,
It was the place your world came crashing down,
When you saw rabbits could even be brown,
Driving by that place, I always wear a smile,
It grows on me, as I cross my historic mile,
The patio is bigger now; the view as well has changed,
More organized though, seems like time has just fled.
—*Giridhar Deviramma Jaded*

Mother nature

Why bother picking up a gun,
Instead, gather some harmless fun,
Why bother giving in to hate,
Instead, change someone's fate.
Why bother giving in to greed,
Instead, help someone in need.
Why bother giving in to war,
Instead of easing someone's scar.
Why bother fighting for power,
Instead of uniting and growing taller.
Why bother giving in to violence,
Instead of understanding emotions.
Why bother being cold to others,
Instead, share the warmth; it matters.
Why bother building mansions in the future,
Instead of living amidst Mother Nature.
—*Giridhar Kashibai Jaded*

Stopped counting days

The days that I keep counting,
I wonder what I am really wanting,
Is it my dreams, or is it my hunger?
Or is it just another passing thunder?
I wonder, I wonder, and I wonder,
About everything I have, and also yonder.
My thoughts are free, and so am I,
My heart's my engine, my mind - its alibi.
There's a strange aura that surrounds destiny,
Encapsulating – like an alluringly sweet mystery,
Where I am headed, is not my choice,
Something drives me, and I am under its vice,
I play along, and I write a song,
If life's long, why not just sing along?
I have stopped counting days by now,
Reinventing ways to be good, and how.
—*Giridhar Manohar Jaded*

One fine day

I am neither a master nor a slave,

My words and thoughts are all what life reluctantly gave.

I don't own it, nor do I give in,

There's a parallel reality that I dispel in,

Existence is not just on the outside,

More like what we feel inside,

I have this battle that never ends,

A camaraderie with my innermost feelings,

I am vulnerable yet unexposed,

But my thoughts do flow unopposed,

I bring out some, I also hide a few,

This love affair with words, I always knew.

I am someone looking for that meaning,

To my reflection in a mirror, quite beckoning,

I will rattle on until the very day,

Till I find my answers one fine day.

—*Giridhar Padma Jaded*

A morning walk

An early morning shower, nice and warm,
Washing away worries from yesterday's storms.
A steely look in the mirror, staring back,
No time to be lazy or hit the sack.
I dab on some deodorant, get in my sneakers,
Put on my earphones, for music in my ears.
I lock the door and step on out,
There's the morning sun but also the cold.
But aren't we all used to acts colder?
From people, from actions, young and the elder?
Which is worse, the answer is yours to find,
What's in putting your body through a little grind,
Sometimes I run, sometimes I just walk,
Music in my ears, I also let my mind talk,
A rainbow here, a Turtle there, at times I get to watch,
The bliss from a morning walk is hard to match.

—*Giridhar Linganagouda Jaded*

Tales of a Guitar

Strings from a Guitar, they do tell a tale,
Some shining bright, some worn, looking pale.
A tale of rigor unlike none other,
With sounds inside, the strings still flutter.
Flutter they will, only when there's a fight,
From an artist trying to find his or her might,
It takes courage to make them ring,
Let alone the pleasure in making them sing,
Feeding off passion, music ain't easy,
Takes soul searching to nail a melody.
Chords become your best of buddies,
Failed attempts also create memories,
Which strings make a song, and which don't?
Is on the artist who knows his or her worth,
What's that song you are strumming,
That will one day, be hard to not keep humming.

—Giridhar Geeta Jaded

Lost in your smile

You make me sing a song,
Or rather just play along,
You make my eyes glisten,
Wanting to forever listen,
To your laughter mild or wild,
Can't get you off my mind,
You make me ride the blues,
Or rather help me keep my dues,
You make my smile widen,
Yeah - I crave for you now, often.
Craving for your presence beside me,
Because you make me feel like me.
You make me wanna walk tall,
Not afraid anymore of a thumping fall,
You make my world come alive,
Come closer now, wanna be lost in your smile.
—*Giridhar Vijayalakshmi Jaded*

A week that went by

On a Sunday morning, we woke up and walked along,
And by evening you knew my favorite songs.
On a Monday morning, we woke up,
With a headache from not sleeping much.
We texted all night long and by now,
You knew my favorite people and how,
On a Wednesday evening, we had dinner,
Spent laughing and fighting over a winner,
On who knows more about metrosexuals,
My mind still fresh with those visuals.
On Thursday morning, we woke up together,
Skipped work, spent a day getting wilder.
On Friday, we had our first argument,
Tempers flared; comments were exchanged.
Come Saturday, there was radio silence,
I won't lie, I can still feel your presence.
—*Giridhar Ashok Jaded*

Who worked them weeds?

Those seeds of hurt that were sown,
Grew into proportions previously unknown.
Forming an uncomfortable knot inside of me,
Pea-sized yet nurturing demonic dreams, like a wannabe.

Those seeds of silence that were sown,
Turned into howling blizzards on their own.
Whistling on silent nights in my ears,
Awakening demons and my deepest fears.

Those seeds of distrust that were sown,
Turned into blisters - ugly and outgrown.
Erupting in silence occasionally, then full blown,
At times causing a grimace, other times a frown.

Those seeds of ignorance that were sown.
Grew into walls I look back at, and scorn,
I wonder who planted all those seeds,
Was it me and you caught up in deeds?
Or was it someone else yonder worked the weeds?
—*Giridhar Ramanagouda Jaded*

Legacy I leave behind

Walking amongst these tipsy curves,
Brimming with ideas and silent thoughts,
I look ahead, and I see plenty a turn,
Some lush green, laid with glistening urns,
Some coated in gold, some rugged and old,
Some treacherous, some mysterious and cold,
Some hideous, whilst some plainly obnoxious,
Some reeking of pain, some whimsical and magnanimous.

Perched I am right now, lost as well as found,
Which road is mine to walk around?
I climb on a rock, trying to be smart,
To see far ahead, and all I see is dark,
I close my eyes and take a spin,
Praying for guidance, as my mind's in a tailspin,
Pray I do, for no matter what way I go,
The legacy I leave behind inspires a life or two.

—*Giridhar Anysuya Jaded*

Respect for Life

A homeless man perched on the road,
In a tweed jacket rugged and old,
Trying to smile, despite shivering in the cold,
Invoke empathy for money, he'd been told.
He knew not much but to be kind,
Ignored the advice and smiled in his mind,
His eyes hid many a story untold,
Of warmth from the world, but more from cold.
He was a residue of his own past,
Mistakes were small, the repercussions were vast,
Acceptant he was to where he stood now,
But one stinging pain, hard to let go,
It was from the looks he got all around,
Of mistrust-filled eyes, even when he smiled on out.
He looks up and says,
"I beg for a living now, yes, I became a homeless,
Don't look down on me; I have self-respect, other things I care less".
—*Giridhar Subhash Jaded*

Please do holler

Is there a place somewhere?
Far from agony and despair,
Where birds flap wings with glee,
And all hearts are just set free?

Is there a place somewhere?
Far from treachery and hatred,
Where the stars come down and dance,
Seducing one and all, in a happy trance?

Is there a place somewhere?
Far from greed and flimsy human needs,
Where compassion is at every street,
Hugs are warm and true indeed?

Is there a place somewhere?
Far from violence and bloodshed,
Where peace is at every corner?
If you find that place, please do holler.
—*Giridhar Myna Jaded*

Gather some scars

I wonder what is that place,
Where all my demonic fears rest?
If I knew, I would walk up there,
Holding a boisterous, raging flame,
And toss it while they hideously sleep,
And hear them cry and weep.
They have cut into my flesh so deep,
No mercy on haters, I can watch them bleed,
I don't look away from the cries, I stand and watch,
The vibes I feel from it, hard to match,
They put up a fight, a rather brave one,
Giving me more than a few sideburns,
I stand basking in front of raging flames, unfazed,
Admiring the beauty emanating from my blaze,
Now my fears are few, by and far,
But I am glad and it was a good way to gather some scars.
—*Giridhar Vasundhara Jaded*

Let me be in harmony

At times a wish in my exotic mind,
Is for the demons residing in my mind,
With me being captive in their bind,
For they are mean, not even randomly never kind.
Playing with my confidence,
Toying even my subconscious,
Trying to ruin my conscience,
Spoiling my leftover silence.
But a lesson I learned,
Is to not give up on a fight,
There shall be scars alright,
Back off now or face my might.
My fists are now bloody,
Apparently beat up one too many,
Go now, let me be in harmony,
Or enjoy the bashing ceremony.
—*Giridhar Shrikant Jaded*

The good things

If you unlocked the door to your soul,
Let me wander into your core,
And find my place in your depths,
Until I rest myself in peace.
I am not afraid of the dark,
Nor from the imminent scars,
If at all I would help them heal,
Nothing more surreal than being real.
I know what I find out there,
Could be a story of hurt and despair,
But I wanna give it my all, and be fair,
You are not alone, it's now OUR pain.
I shall be unfazed by what I find,
Togetherness is all that's on my mind.
C'mon now kick the door open,
Good things happen when allowed to happen.
—*Giridhar Pavan Jaded*

A silent Goodbye

When you look back at those times,
Those aimless walks and countless smiles,
And the unending fights then went on,
The caterpillars that just crawled on,
Gnawing at our stonewalled trust,
Breaking a tooth or two at first,
But slowly heeded by our doubts,
They began a digging of our souls.
We let them in, we had our chance,
To not let them disrupt this blissful trance.
When you look back at those moments,
What is it that you see?
Is it the pain or the love in my eyes?
Is it the laughter or the unending silence?
It's what you see now that will define,
If we walk along or bid a silent Goodbye.

—*Giridhar Apoorva Jaded*

A sky — lovely blue

On life's crossroads, once in a while,

In moments spent over elongated time,

That flew past without caring a dime,

We all stand, like puppets in a mime,

Finding ways to forge our next big move,

Strong enough to last years, least a few,

It's moments like these that define us,

And whether we hop into or miss the bus,

It's always a hard choice to make,

To trust thy heart or your nimble brain,

Choose your way, the one making most sense,

One way from experience, the other is to experience.

If it was me making the choice,

I am always gonna go by my heart,

For experiences make us feel something new,

Less I see dark or a sky — lovely blue.

—*Giridhar Prashanth Jaded*

A Saturday night wish

Last Saturday night, on the altar,
We had a lovely kiss, under the stars.
I saw the mountains in lush green and yellow,
Feet off the ground, my heart went mellow.
We had no plans, but we had a night,
Like a scented candle next to a light.
Unless struck, the candle cannot shine,
It could have ended as just another night.
That very night, you told me a wish,
Tossing and turning, I haven't slept since.
If your little wish is, to me a big fish,
I will soon be an insomniac lost in you, miss.
Every flower in the world has a wish,
To rise high and blow the skies a gentle kiss.
I ain't a genie, but I know this much,
If you are into me, I will be into you as much.

—*Giridhar Madhura Jaded*

Hide and Seek

There's a hide and seek that we all play,
With ourselves and the dreams we carry.
Dreams, like clouds, do get blown away,
If you let them loose, or just look away.
Like a nimble deer can't stand its ground,
Dreams are like toddlers, fickle-mind bound.
They need to be caught, and nurtured,
Or they wither away, into another world,
Where someone else awaits a steal,
To transform your dreams into something real.
Catch yours before it's too late,
To not be left standing, cursing your fate.
Hide and seek is a tantalizing game,
Play it with dreams and you got yourself to blame.
Dare to dream and strive to make them real,
Either you walk tall, or you kneel down and squeal.

—*Giridhar Mridula Jaded*

Flights to catch

I like it when your eyes light up,

When you talk about the things that matter.

The dreams that you delectably carry,

In your basket lined with roses and strawberries,

Like saplings, you water them daily,

Belief - your wings, doubts - a mere anomaly,

To fly is an eternal wish of every soul,

What's a soccer field without a goal?

You don't like soccer, but you very well know,

Without a kick, there isn't any goal.

Wear your high heels or your comfy flats,

Together we have many a flight to catch,

If anything, I will be the spark in your eyes,

To be your light in your darker days.

Dream on my love, light up the world,

I'll protect them - with words as my armor and my sword.

—*Giridhar Kiran Jaded*

A wordless world

Words can be like birds,

Flying high or laying low.

Words can be like nerds,

Shining bright or a pale some glow,

Words can be like spears,

Painfully sparkling or lackluster and dull.

Words can be like oceans,

Enormous in sight, yet daunting inside,

Words can be like a potion,

Heal a life or poison it,

Words can be like droplets,

Calming when gentle, stinging when fierce.

Words can be like magnets,

Drawing you in or pushing you away.

Words are words until heard or read,

A world without words, to think itself, is dread.

—*Giridhar Tejraj Jaded*

Everything's gonna be alright

I feel these vibes around you,
Eternally sweet, pure and true.
Making me flutter on the inside,
Making me 'me'- nothing to hide.

I feel these vibes around you,
Blissfully deep, uplifting and new.
Making me driven on the inside,
Making me 'me' - ready to ride.

I feel these vibes around you,
Passionately right, glittery and new.
Making me go jello' on the inside,
Making me 'me' - love blind.

I feel these vibes around you,
Dreamy-eyed, positive and so you,
Making me stronger on the inside,
Vibe on - everything's gonna be alright.
—*Giridhar Naveen Jaded*

I Love You

Is there no place else for you?
Then spaces in my empty mind?
You fill my conscience with thoughts,
Some beautiful, some totally new.
Is there no place else for you?
Then the bottom of my heart?
You fill my heart with dreams,
Some surreal, some wild and blue.
Is there no place else for you?
Then the dark places I hide?
You fill me with lightning flashes,
Some enlightening, some painfully true.
Is there no place else for you?
Then the depths of my soul?
You fill me with a purpose.
Just wanna say – I love you.

—*Giridhar Nitin Jaded*

My #1 Radio station

You are the radio of my life,

My flashback, my jukebox and my Live.

The songs you playlist for me,

There's nowhere else I'd seek,

You know I like the blues,

and songs to bring out my moves.

You know I like Mr. Bryan Adams,

and the sound of a Guitar with drums.

You fill my life with melody,

You Rock my blues away.

You touch my core with classics,

Baby, you know my perfect mix.

You sense my mood and play a song,

I feel the love and hum along.

I smile, for I never use the tune button,

You are my #1 radio station.

—Giridhar Nandan Jaded

Of failed love

Silence became a routine,
Between a couple madly in love,
Outbursts became a routine,
Between a couple idolized before,
The ocean of love that lived,
Between their mighty sacred seas,
Seemed to vanish into thin air,
Cries of anguish in utter despair.
Two beautiful angels, symbols of love,
Watched things change, and how,
Mum and Dad are acting, they assumed at first,
Slowly though, reality began to strike,
Angels are now grown-up teens,
Still half made, half baked, perplexed beings,
Never physically beaten, yet mentally fractured,
Victims of failed love, without falling in love.
—*Giridhar Deepthi Jaded*

Human crabs

Human crabs, I see them around,
Clinging to each-other with pointed claws,
No real dreams, no real goals,
Living lives off empty shoals.

Human crabs they feed off a fall,
Caused by gnawing at someone's paws,
No real passion, no real will,
Finding joy in a push, pull or even a kill.

Human crabs, they are mean and evil,
Feeding off envy, apathy, and greed,
No real whims, no real fantasies,
Leading lives in misfit anomalies.

Human crabs they are dangerous,
Feeding off power, pain, misery on paths treacherous,
Unaware that those very claws,
Can as well strum some soulful songs.
—*Giridhar Abhishek Jaded*

What legacy?

Some smile from their heart,
Some smile to play their part,
Some smile to hide their hurt,
Some smile like there's no tomorrow,
Some hug like they mean it,
Some hug like they need it,
Some hug like they have to,
Some hug like there's no tomorrow.

Some live lives trying to fit in,
Some have hands meant to pitch in,
Some live lives with aplomb,
Some live like there's no tomorrow,
Some die with a smile,
Some die with pain,
Some die – albeit in vain,
Some just leave a legacy behind.

—*Giridhar Shwetha Jaded*

Victim of my inner self

The places I would never go,
If I had a little say,
Into places that my mind wanders,
To spaces dark, haunted and persistent thunder.

The regrets I would never keep,
If I had a little say,
In what my actions meant,
To people around, good and bad.

The tears I would never weep,
If I had a little say,
In how my heart behaved,
Bringing joy or a heartache instead.

The forgiveness I would never ask,
If I had a little say,
In what my mind really wanted,
I'm after all a victim of my inner self.
—Giridhar Avinash Jaded

Pay my rent on time

If there is ever a place,
Where a right is an absolute right,
Take me there will you?
I have a few questions for you.

If there is ever a place,
Where the light just shines bright,
Take me there will you?
Light and dark are siblings, in my view.

If there is ever a place,
Where every fleeting thought is justified,
Take me there will you?
My mind could use some rest.

If there is ever a place,
Where only happiness resides,
Take me there will you?
I shall pay my rent on time, I promise.
—*Giridhar Pratik Jaded*

And how

The wine glasses we together broke,
The teddy bear we tried to choke,
The carpet we set ablaze,
While playing those innocent games,
What do you see when you look back?
Is it broken pieces, or a picture - dark?
Is it a beautiful place, or a shattered raft?
You can't deny we played a lot.
The light bulbs that we changed,
From long nights of being awake in bed.
Do you still feel any warmth?
Or did we then summon a cloud, dark?
Those games from before that were really fun,
Replaced now with games of gloom and glum,
Was it worth it, only back then? Or is it now?
Strange how life throws questions at us, and how.
—*Giridhar Karthik Jaded*

No date on tomorrow

Let's go to a place beautiful and shallow,
Where there's no date on tomorrow,
Where the days are just days,
And the nights vibe in the right ways,
Where there ain't no race against the clock.
Tick Tock Tick Tock Tick Tock,
Where there is no sense of time,
Yet every moment is pure and sublime,
Let's go to a place today, not tomorrow,
Where there's no date on tomorrow,
Where there are more moments than numbers,
After all, a calendar is just a piece of paper,
I ask myself; how do I get there?
A voice whispers back, *'Did you search your inner lair?'*
—*Giridhar Rashmi Jaded*

Seek beyond

Some nights I lay wide awake,
Not really thinking about mansions to make,
Or about life's hurdles, yet to face.
Think I do about how can I be, in grace?
I ask questions to please myself,
I ask questions to ease myself,
And when the answers are hard to find,
I pack questions aside and start over again.
With eyes closed, I traverse into a new realm,
Where I converse with myself, in words simple and clean,
Funny it is when my thoughts transform,
Into a frown, laugh, or even a squirm.
I don't suffer from a lack of sleep,
I suffer from what's called 'thinking deep,'
In things that you seek to seek beyond,
Answers lay to all questions, big or small.

—*Giridhar Preethi Jaded*

A stranger on the Bus

A stranger on the bus, he was weird.
Striking up conversations is all he did,
He was flamboyant, had a purposeful look,
Men like him, usually carry around a book,
He smiled at everyone on every single ride,
Making one wonder if that's how he earned in life,
He seemed in no rush and always got off last.
After talking to a few strangers on the bus.
One fine day after he left, I had to ask,
The driver of the bus, as to what all this was about?
He smiled back and with a heavy voice,
Told me a story on how love can survive,
This man was grumpy, sad, and an ego child,
At least that how he was, for most of his life,
Fate though took away his loved ones in a crash,
In her dying moments, his Love had pleaded and asked,
To be nice to strangers, ones riding on a bus called life,
For life can create strangers even with people around,
And if nothing, everyone can use another caring arm.

—Giridhar Kashi Nath Jaded

My naked mile

I call out your name a million times,
Every time I remember your radiant smile.
And each time I have felt that chill,
In moments I spend missing you - still.

I call out your name a million times,
Each time I walk or run a mile.
And each time that I feel the cold,
From this world, even then I try to be bold.

I call out your name a million times,
Each time I miss your positive vibes.
And each time I hit a unsolvable riddle,
I look up to you, to steady me from my wobble.

I call out your name a million times,
Each time I ponder over life for a while.
And each time I feel I have forgotten to smile,
I look up to you and continue walking my naked mile.

—*Giridhar Kiran Jaded*

The city of love

Raindrops sparkling in the morning sun.

Was it a sign of something good to come?

Someone seemed to have sprinkled hope all around,

As every single soul seemed to walk northbound.

The rainbow fit into the morning like a charm,

Her colors painted a canvas nice and warm,

Being kind to one another for a change, seemed the norm,

Everyone was welcomed with open arms,

The homeless had shelter and food, wore a smile warm,

Every action was loaded with an intent of good.

Reality seemed more blissful than a fantasy from Hollywood,

The politics of life and work, nowhere to be seen,

But this haven was restricted just one city,

Every place else still suffered from reality.

A love bomb had been dropped in the night,

On this city that found a new way towards light.

—*Giridhar Kotish Jaded*

Note: Let's build cities of love & give back to villages what we owe.

Maternal return

That moment when a baby is born,
A Mom instinctively forgets how to frown.
That moment when a baby blissfully smiles,
A Mom loses her every sense of time.

That moment when a baby starts to walk,
A Mom is a second shadow at the back,
That moment a baby becomes a child,
A Mom protects, prepares it for the grind.

That moment a child turns into an adult,
A Mom is a shoulder on which they rest.
That moment her loved one is broken,
A Mom fixes the heart, like a magician.
From diapers, to sickness, to tantrums,
A Mom stands by, through all the seasons,
That moment when you think of your Mom,
Do YOU wonder if you've been your best in return?
—*Giridhar Aanshi Jaded*

Think out loud

Broken wings, ugly scars,
Veil of darkness, distant stars.
Restless heart, sleepless nights,
Rustic talks, endless fights.
Lonely screams, violent dreams,
Uninvited demons, scary realms.
Frozen emotions, oceans of emptiness,
A constant battle of loneliness.
Lacking conviction lost affection,
Unsaid words, unending inhibitions.
Missed chances, routine rants,
Scornful regrets, senseless wants.
Part of these or all of these,
At some point in life, don't we all feel?
In such moments - breathe, and think out loud,
If others have been here and gotten out, how do I bail out?
—*Giridhar Ananya Jaded*

Behind that veil

Is there a pleasure unknown?
That mankind has never sown,
Seems unfathomable to think at least,
In chasing pleasures, aren't we humans a beast?
From lavish mansions to exotic islands,
From private jet planes to life coaches,
From exotic cars to mind-numbing gadgets,
In feeding desires, aren't we the best?
Chasing fame to moments of shame,
Giving in to lust to letting souls rust,
A mouthful of deceit, to the sins concealed,
From wanting things to wanting things,
We have a heart, impossible to not feel,
And to act on what we feel,
But once in a while behind that omnipresent veil,
It's good to think a little, about how we make others feel.

—Giridhar Amit Jaded

To feel alive

I had days' worth hating,
I had days' worth fearing,
I had days' worth not wanting,
I had days' worth nothing.
Gone are those days of hiding,
Gone are the days of doubting,
Gone are the days of suffering,
Gone are the days of ranting.
Now my days are bearable,
Now my days are cheerful,
Now my days are eventful,
Now my days are hopeful.
I want my days to fight fire,
I want my days to inspire,
I want my days to feel alright,
I want my days to feel alive.

—*Giridhar Deepak Jaded*

Locked out thoughts

I think my mind works in circles,
Or it doesn't know what listening means.
It keeps going back to locked out thoughts,
Finding keys hidden from within my knots,
I wonder from where it gets its girth,
To challenge thy master, for what's worth,
And then like a stubborn child, it runs away,
To places I'd not even lose my way,
If there is so much hidden out there,
Luring it into submission, wandering away,
How is it I shall keep my mind at bay?
Or shall I hustle on, come what may?
Then another thought crosses my heart,
And my mind picks on it like an inspiration of Art,
Unlocking a lock, I had so tightly wrapped,
Circling me back to where I had a start.
—*Giridhar Prashanth Jaded*

What am I to you?

How do you see me?
For who I am when fully clothed,
Or when stark naked, and exposed?

How do you judge me?
From my actions in the dark,
Or my deeds in broad daylight?

How do you like me?
For who I am while I search,
Or who I will be when I find myself?

How do you feel me?
Like how I feel deep inside,
Or rather a mysterious vibe?

How do you love me?
Is it for who I am,
Or for I shall become?
—*Giridhar Krishna Jaded*

On the other side

Sometimes when I open doors,
I see myself switching corridors.
Even in the most absurd of settings,
I find myself switching horizons.
The concrete beneath becomes green grass,
I find myself shoeless walking softened lawns,
The sounds around cease to exist,
The calmness in the air, hard to resist,
I love flirting, albeit with my thoughts,
Such conversations when deep are like gold.
I fade away losing a sense of time,
Until jolted back to reality by someone around,
Losing my train of thought from the other side,
I smile, nod, and get back with the tide.
These moments barely last a few seconds in time,
Yet leave a lot to be felt in mystical moments that shine,
I wonder if others also have moments like these,
And how would it be to meet on the other side?

—*Giridhar Sudha Jaded*

Irony of things

A dirty sock of her love, unwashed,

Sweaty t-shirt of Mom as pillow, unwashed,

A Chivas Regal for Dad, unopened,

Two years have passed, yet a son's Lego house stays intact.

The socks he wore the day he died,

Mom's smell as comfort, a long year of separation ahead,

A feeling of a drink together, with Dad,

The pride at seeing that Lego house.

There's no pain like being away,

From ones departed or ones gone a while,

The pain shall be less, if instead of things,

Togetherness is treasured, in moments spent as caring beings.

—Giridhar Shobha Jaded

Walks in the park

When you silently turn and walk away,
My mind is inventing a way to say,
A genuine sorry, in a different way,
Because what I said till now didn't sway.
I've a dictionary in my mind, but sometimes,
I grope around dangling worldly vines.
My mind stutters when I am nervous,
About something, about someone intense.
I am more like myself when I am calm,
You already have danced to my mystic charm.
No two trees have ever grown the same,
Difference minuscule, even different in veins.
So, hang on please, the next time around,
For a while, we shall sit; not a sound.
And then my love, we shall talk,
Like we do on those walks in the park.

—*Giridhar Shilpa Jaded*

Random Thoughts

Some people are really mixed up in unexplainable ways. The world out there isn't easy. It's at times, unsparingly nasty.

Don't be surprised if you are accused of breaking the same ideals that you ever so affectionately lived by. The same principles that you carry on your shoulders with pride will be tied to your tail with a dirty broom as if to remind, that when the minds of some get perplexed, logic kind of finds its way out the window.

Hang tight and smile on. Realization dawns late for some. Hope they as well catch on. You fight on.

—*Giridhar Kittu (Pramod) Jaded*

A perfect adventure

As life goes on, as the seasons change,
If the trail you are on is right,
You will see yourself grow, alright,
Or probably fail to notice that changes are featherlight.
But, if you veer and look close enough,
The tides will align with your surf,
And crystal clear you shall see,
You are far ahead of where you used to be.
A lure from your past is now a fleeting thought,
A worry from your past, been chased on out,
Scars from your past, now faded and light,
Find those nimble changes, you will feel alright.
When the going gets tough, just sit tight,
Scrounge your past, there is always light,
If you are a thrill seeker, life is a perfect adventure,
Just be a rough rider, and in time, the demons do surrender.
—*Giridhar Sunil Jaded*

A bloody you

The way you look at me in contempt,
From yourself not being able to compete,
With my raging fire, my positive intent,
You act menacing but your eyes give in, in silence,
That hidden fear behind those layers,
I shall keep you in my prayers.

The way you avoid greeting me,
Proves how daunting I can really be.
For if my presence can make you avoid,
My whole will destroy you, leave a void.
I have nothing but empathy for you,
But I know to always see a battle through.
So, the choice is yours, c'mon now,
It's either a hug or an exchange of blows.
Before you make a choice, good luck to you,
It'll be drinks together, or goodbye to a bloody you.

—*Giridhar Mamatha Jaded*

Dreams that rust

Sordid tales of dreams that rust,
Eyes greedy for wanderlust.
Broken wings and vanquished nests,
Weary eyes that know no rest.
Crawling emotions, totally lost.
Broken hearts, at what cost?
Castles of greed, as one's nest,
Weary souls, an empathy fest.
Wayward paths, filled with rocks,
Suspicious eyes, looking to mock.
Demons galore, a sumptuous feast,
On souls weak giving in to those beasts.
Is life a maze, so hard to cross?
Gnawing each other – who's at a loss?

—Giridhar Suresh Jaded

Abundance of Life

What is it that's so compelling to you?
That blinds all the good things around you?
What is it that encapsulates you?
Creating an aura of mystique around you?
Where is it that you seem utterly lost?
Is it a distant dream or a thing from the past?
Where is it that you keep looking?
What's in your mind, persistently brewing?
Unless I know, I shall be a nobody,
Once I do, I'll try to make a good somebody.
Answer these what's and where's and trust me,
No dream solution is an impossible reality,
Silence is meaningful only when mutual,
Seeking help isn't a forbidden ritual.
Good things transpire when you talk,
Life's abundance isn't meant for a lonely walk.

—*Giridhar Shashan Jaded*

My Bestseller

If you were a book, waiting to be opened,
I would flip your pages with my mind,
Deftly, so as to not leave behind,
A blotch or a fold of the ugly kind.

I would dive deep and try to find,
The lessons that would really blow my mind.
I would take my time reading you,
And see my perception grow around you.

I would link your thoughts with those of mine,
Making mental notes, for later to rewind,
If you were a book, filled with wisdom,
Would you mind being a Queen in my kingdom?

I would pretend to suffer from amnesia,
To wake up in your arms, from anesthesia.
I am in love with the act of reading,
Will you then be my bestseller in the making?

—*Giridhar Sunil Jaded*

A doorway sky bound

Invisible shards of restraint,
Incorrigible people, not saints.
Superfluous words, in a bind,
Perplexed souls, in a grind.
Uneventful days, on rewind,
Abundance in life, hard to find.
An empty night, hollow and unkind,
A lost soul, body, and the mind.
Peaceful moments, hard to find,
No place in time, to unwind.
Agony aunt finding a home,
In hearts wanting love like in Rome.
A hard look inside, and also around,
A possible doorway, sky bound,
Thoughtful decisions, well-timed, well-thought,
Half a battle won even before the start.

—*Giridhar Sharath Jaded*

Moving on

When I wait for your phone call,
I know I am on an unending fall,
Into an abyss infinitely deep and dark,
Treacherous, slippery, and also stark.

When I wait for your text,
I know I am not thinking at all,
For if I was, history had it all,
I knew which of the demons stood tall.
I seem to enjoy a dive,
Once in a while, in my life,
Where reason is an unknown entity,
While I try to find my sanctity.
I have all the time to keep waiting,
And I've decided to use it for something,
Something sacred to my inner soul,
Solace is also hidden in moving on.
—*Giridhar Rakesh Jaded*

The blinking cursor

The cursor on my cell phone, it blinks,
Nonchalantly as my mind thinks.
Sometimes the blinker stares at me,
Trying to hide a raw, poignant, mockery.
Sometimes the blinking is replaced by a stoic,
If a thought comes running to me in a panic.
Other times the blinking is omnipresent,
Making me look for a way to vent.
So, vent I do against the blinking cursor,
Channeling my thoughts, also my anger,
Fascinating a battle it is, every single time,
Victory - a poem written; Loss - lost time.
The truth though, is that every time I stare at the cursor,
I am one step closer to being a good writer.

—*Giridhar Praveen Jaded*

Beyond the mountains

Behind those pristine mountains,
Seen through these lacy curtains,
There's an experience unknown,
With its roots in my heart and soul.

Beneath the voices of the chirping birds,
Music to the ears, even on the days that are hard,
There's an experience unknown,
Waiting on my decision, one of my own.

Below the shades of the lush green trees,
Resides an unfelt moment of peace,
Willing to come so far along,
And embrace me in its open arms.

Between these experiences and my lives,
Is an unending, ugly, violent fight,
A fight that rages in my willing mind,
Either I live them, or curl up in bed, to hide.

—*Giridhar Vishal Jaded*

A better place to be

If life was a scented candle,
What would you rather be?
Would you be the tender wax?
Boiling itself to spread the scent,
Or rather the skinny wick?
That burns itself to spread the light,
Both have their part to play,
Whilst one takes the darkness away,
The other makes your senses sway,
Whilst one vanishes into thin air,
The other holds, hoping for repair,
Together, they make a perfect pair.
Whichever you choose is unto thee,
Try making the world a better place to be.

—Giridhar Ravi Jaded

Someone to hang on to

What is pain after everything ceases,
From emptiness in the heart that releases?
What is the big deal about a heartache?
Does it cause you to stop your breath?
Do you stop living after a broken heart?
You will still do what you really want,
You will still have your daily lunch,
A broken heart isn't really a punch.
A soul is nothing but a sacred experience,
To pass on to them oncoming generations,
Look beyond a life of broken hearts,
There's hope in everything around, in parts,
Find something, not someone, to hang on to,
And life shall find a way to scrape through.

—*Giridhar Gokul Jaded*

The lessons learnt

The moments of goosebumps in your life,
Aren't limited to only happy times,
There are goosebumps felt even when you're sad,
Even after having done something bad.
But what you learn from those moments,
You become a new you or a stockpile of hurts,
Beyond an experience is always a lesson,
Learned only when you nail the real reason,
Let those butterflies fly in the air,
You are giving yourself a chance, it's just fair.
What's a heart that doesn't really hurt?
If life's too fair, you will have no lessons learned.
So, take a chill pill and enjoy the moment,
Just try not to do something you will utterly lament.
—*Giridhar Prashanth Jaded*

Someone more

What is life without a few gasps,
Of breath from moments good and bad,
Without experiences that make us feel alive?

What is life without a few missed chances,
That uphold the power of hopefulness,
Without the urge to make some progress?

What is life without a few heartaches,
That makes you stronger on the inside,
Without a heart that yearns for love?

What is life without a few chest-thumps?
That defines your defining moments,
Without a real urge to succeed?

What is life without a few adventures,
That overcome some of your fears,
Without an urge to be someone more?
—*Giridhar Kiran Jaded*

The dung beetles

Two cups of tea in the morning,
Sounds like a very trivial thing,
Happiness is for those who are looking within,
Beyond the line of sight, deep inside,
Gestures in life are like dung beetles,
Serving hearts, ignored, often unnoticeable,
Togetherness in life is like a shadow,
Fighting the loneliness beast in its shallows,
The gesture of having a morning drink,
Even with empty mugs is a nice feeling,
It's the gestures, the lovely dung beetles,
That shall fill life with more meaning, even in trickles,
Buy your mugs, pick a trail, or just set sail,
Only by riding on gestures, shall love live to prevail.

—*Giridhar Sandeep Jaded*

I too am a beast

There's not much hate left in me I guess,
But deep inside, I carry an ocean of hate,
Only for the ugly demon named 'Excuse,'
Who tries to crush my spirit; making recluses.
As nagging as he is, indomitably persistent,
With arms of rustic steel, damn he's resilient.
He knocks on my door ever so often,
Stares at me with lustful eyes that glisten.
Either I lay here in bed, shivering inside,
And put up a bold face, hoping he'll recede,
Or I do the right thing, that I often don't,
Go full throttle, to then leave him on the floor.
He towers over me in shape and size,
But good things come to those who fight,
You might be a demon, but I too am a beast,
Not shy of turning your excuses into a feast.
—*Giridhar Vinayak Jaded*

The ultimate sacrifice

The millions of lives that were lost,
The thousands that shall again be lost,
Conflict and war, they depict a sordid story,
For the future, in the present, from history.
Opinions are the roots that nurture conflict,
Watered by a lust for power, with an ego twist,
Not all lives lost are in vain; in fact, they may be necessary,
Bitter truth - cruelly calling it necessary.
Some lives are lost to defeat the unjust,
Or to crush the ugly hood of unrest.
But spare a thought for those lost lives,
Or the loved ones they left behind.
What's it like to play hide and seek?
With impending death, yet not be weak.
—*Giridhar Ramakrishna Jaded*

A meekly smile

I hear feathers ruffling on my inside,
Tingling my senses, causing them to wildly glide,
I feel twitches forming on my inside,
Rankled from a plethora of desires.

I see shapes forming on my inside,
Created from experiences of all kinds,
I sense a tsunami of feelings on my inside,
Erupting as words I attempt to coin.

I listen to these voices from my inside,
Voices that have never known to subside,
What I feel is just a part of my inside,
If my words strike a chord, I'll be insanely glad,

Even if my simple thoughts do inspire,
A creation of Art more glorious than mine,
I shall do nothing but acknowledge and smile,
For in some little way, I have been worthwhile.

—*Giridhar Daniel Jaded*

Heart made of gold

The lip gloss that you elegantly wear,
The shining bow in your pitch-black hair,
The sex appeal you sprinkle in the air,
That jaywalk that you effortlessly nail,
The oomph in your every single inch,
Ain't lying - you could make any man flinch.

The magic you weave with your eyes,
The fantasies that you induce with your smiles.
If beauty were a ship, you would be the Titanic,
If beauty were the devil, you would be the Satan.
If beauty were a priest, you would be an Angel,
If beauty were water, you would be an Ocean.

But I can't seem to find the reason,
As to how your heart, once made of gold,
Got so hardened, frozen in layers of cold,
Leaving a trail of broken hearts on the road.
—*Giridhar Vikas Jaded*

Drifted too far

There's mystique in your eyes, I won't lie,
My heart flutters like a hummingbird when you smile.
A hundred suiters for you still wanna try,
'Try' is a small word, I would rather dive.

There's an enigma in you that's like a high,
There's a stigma in you like a broken heart's cry.
There's an air bout you, making me wanna fly,
There's a class in you like seasoned rye.

Your choice of perfumes, oh my gosh,
Your cute arrogance, oh my gosh,
When I see you, I imagine a pristine river,
With a hazy mist, and absolute eerie wonder.
I see a boat I am dying to jump on,
But something in me says 'hold on.'
What if you are one of those, angels only from far?
With a heart that's dark, having drifted too far?
—*Giridhar Swaminath Jaded*

Spaces of time

When you lay in bed, lost in thought,
Always remember this little part,
From a story that I brewed in my mind,
When searching for some answers, hard to find.

A boy once lived in a small little town,
Aged ten, yet had a face glued to a frown,
Tender his age, but not the hardships he faced,
Tender his skin, his heart was over-baked.

He mastered an art - being lost in thought,
Often about his haunting past.
It made his heart bleed ounce by ounce,
Until one day he gnawed back and pounced.

He sleeps well now, really because,
He made a final peace with his past,
And those spaces of time lost in thought,
Now filled mostly by positive parts.

—Giridhar Vineet Jaded

Have a good day

Rustic thoughts, they come and go,
Sometimes staggered, other times in a flow,
They bring along colors, they bring along flavors,
Sometimes shades of dark, other times bright with fervor,
Sweet at times, bitter as well, in a flow,
Welcome them, sit with them, let them go,
After you have made notes on a thing or two,
Be a master, they your slave, let them go,
But the thoughts that are beautiful and divine,
Catch hold of them, and hook up a line,
To pull a string in those lowly times of yours,
Where you are your worst, battling your fears,
The good ones are good, but they like to play,
Hide and seek – can't afford to lose your way,
Make friends with them – have a good day.

—*Giridhar Amruth Jaded*

For the younger lot

No one is ever born, to not dream on,
Born is everyone for one good reason.
That quest for the reason unknown,
Is won sooner by some, eats up others whole.
Dreams are born when a young mind,
Makes sense of things around and ones inside.
The seeds to fruits that a life shall reap,
I think, are sown somewhere in the teens.

Learn and play away your childhood,
Bake in everything, observe yourself and your hood,
Ask yourself the pertinent question *'In what do I excel?'*
Don't take pity on yourself until its sealed.
Being good at something, to being excellent at something,
Is like two rail tracks with no hopes of meeting.

Once found, dive deep into what you excel at,
Or something you will excel at, with perseverance and time.
The sail ahead isn't going to be smooth,
Chasing your passion, at least you have less to lose.

—*Giridhar Vinit Jaded*

Kindness-Just an act away

The lies that you wrap ever so deftly,

Taking pains to cover the mystery,

Lighting candles to hide treachery,

Wearing a suit to conceal hypocrisy,

Making plans to glorify such a victory,

Weaving a seductive web of tomfoolery,

Have you ever stopped to think?

What drives you and what doesn't?

There might be something mixed up,

Somewhere in your mind, something is out.

Or maybe the way some minds were wired,

Puts them behind amongst the evolutionary kind,

An evolution from being oneself to being kind.

Through being kind, and spreading kindness,

Compassion is just an act away, in essence.

—*Giridhar Prabhu Jaded*

Respect that Woman

The space between a woman's legs,
Is not just to bury your face,
Or to leave behind a hollow space,
Or to openly display your lack of grace,
Or to merely deploy an ounce of yourself.

There's beauty in every piece of nature,
So is beauty in that sacred space you wander,
It paves the way for the emergence of life,
For its from life, hope emanates and then light,
A light that creates dreams and experiences alike,
A creation of a possibility needs to be treated right.

Respect given is respect earned, but,
How many a unsuspecting hearts have been ruptured?
When the intent from men has been misled,
Leaving behind an ocean of hurt and that of dread,
In respect for women lays the respect for nature,
Paving the way towards a beautiful future.
—*Giridhar Shivayogi Jaded*

An ode to Art and artists

The light bulbs glistened in the dark,
Even when the lights were switched off.
The red light from a gadget beckoned,
Miniature in size yet towering over the mind.
Even with eyes closed, the red light blinked,
Voices in the mind, silence-it winked.
In the darkness and silence came a sound - lub-dub,
From a beating heart that wanted a way up,
A Writer got up and picked up a pen,
A Singer got up and picked up a Guitar,
A Painter got up and picked up a brush,
An Actor got up and faced the mirror.
It's when these sleepless souls lay awake,
That magic in the real world, gets to be made.

—*Giridhar Ghanshyam Jaded*

Need, to be freed

I am a citizen of this abundant world,
My eyes don't see lines, nor my flesh feel the cold,
Everywhere I look, I see one need,
A simple basic need to freely breathe.
Breathe oxygen that is, and to seek,
Food and shelter, and a peaceful mind to keep.
A job for all where excellence is sought,
If passion gets aligned - it can be pure bliss.
Life as is, is driven by the need to change,
To find a castle in a sea of mirages.
Raging fires lit mainly from greed.
Fueled by power, an egotist mind's basic need,
Ever wonder about the need to form a creed,
And the sea of change that freedom can help seed,
When the minds are compassion filled and free,
The future is a sky full of stars, where many more smile with glee.
—*Giridhar Shrinivas Jaded*

A bridge of words

The sapling called life given to me,
What's the best way to water it?
Do I water it with hope?
And nurture it with dreams?
Do I water it with fantasies?
Brewing in my mind's factories?
Do I water it with greed?
And get trapped in weeds of need?
Do I sprinkle religion and creed?
Do I water it with kindness?
To myself, loved ones, and ones in need?

How tall and wide can this sapling grow,
The answer is pertinent but resides in a story to be told.
A story in the making, yet to unfold,
All I know is to keep putting a word on word.
—*Giridhar Sumit Jaded*

Unknown cities

An unplanned vacation to a new city,
Lesser known, carrying its own sanctity,
Turned out to be an adventurous ride.
From unexpected nightly cold, on a winter night,
And in between savoring exquisite cuisine by the road,
To visiting a niche boutique, selling torn clothes,
In that shower in a remote cabin somewhere,
I loved the body soap and its earthly flair.

The vacation is long over, but I still have,
The scent and the feeling from that place,
It's a thing worth having, but not like hoarding,
To restock things that help good memories, in rekindling.
If there's an extra room I am allowed to call my own,
I exactly know what shall neatly adorn,
The walls and empty spaces in that room.
Just the memories and fragrances on their own.
—*Giridhar Sambit Jaded*

Note: Inspired by a visit to Fredericksburg, Texas.

The shaming she got

She was more adorable than a puff of cloud,
Her voice so feeble yet inherently bold,
As a toddler, her world was more baby pink,
Not by choice, that's how her Mom liked to think,
She grew up bolder, found her true color,
Was in beauty and painted in yellow fervor,
She set her dreams, knowing very well her strength,
Is in her looks, elegance and her legs, known for length,
She learned to act, was naturally good at drama,
Was resilient by nature, believed in karma,
Life can at times be, a cruel mishap waiting to happen,
Got crucified in an innocent wardrobe malfunction,
A mere crossing of her legs, in innocence,
Made demonic by people, and started out a descent,
She was pronounced lame, too hungry for fame,
To the ones watching, this was another Sunday night game,
For in the comforts of one's own home once,
The very critics lay half naked, more than once,
Had their malfunction even at a public place in hindsight,
But each thanked above for not being in a limelight,
Her dreams intact though, she still has a fight,
To be known as her, not the shaming she got.

—*Giridhar Venugopal Jaded*

Leave the rest aside

The pink scrub that we picked from the store,
To keep immaculately clean, our shower floor,
Says hello to me every single day,
Bringing a frown or a smile on my face.
It's not the choices but the memories made,
That are hung as paintings in life's unending parade,
A faint memory lives in everything around,
Visible only to eyes that look beyond.
I sit in silence, in a corner sometimes,
Wondering if I can scrub some scars off my skin,
Bleach might help, the scars have made a living,
I wonder what to do with the ones in my heart.
The scars that adorn my being, like my own part,
As uncomforting as they were, still taught me a fact,
That's life's a journey best lived,
Picking the good, leaving the rest aside.

—*Giridhar Shivanand Jaded*

Demons in the dark

Sometimes, when falling asleep at night,
I hear rustling and ruffling in the absence of light,
Followed by a mild heart-wrenching moan,
From drooling wolves walking alongside a demon,
There's darkness and a rustic chill in the air,
Smelling of dried blood from a devil's lair.
The moaning grows into a haunting note,
The demon stares, wearing a freshly skinned coat.
Disgusting wardrobe taste, to say the least,
No class, no fragrance, stinking like primitive yeast,
I see his presence, and yearn for his absence,
In my life, there's no room for unwanted stench.
I open doors only when there's some class.
Howl and cry you wolves but try to enter not.
You and your pack look scary, but you know what – you lost the plot,
Dance and howl in your dark, I've got some sleep to catch.

—Giridhar Santosh Jaded

A hopeful song

Those shadows of yours that I captured,
In those pictures that glorified your delight,
And the million poses you proudly struck,
Acknowledging one picture out of a haystack.
I had worries, but more of you in my mind,
I never flinched, I was patient and kind,
Those moments we spent taking pics,
Moments not spent soaking in views,
I don't regret them nor those times,
We made hay while the sun smiled and shined,
I had questions, and now a clear mind,
Can't fathom though, how hard is being kind?
Those shadows have vanished, pictures are gone,
Every day I try humming a hopeful song.

—*Giridhar Ruel Jaded*

A falling leaf

I feel like a falling leaf sometimes,
Drifting from the skies, with no sense of time,
As I hit the atmosphere, I look down and see,
A sea of abundance and possibilities,
I wonder in whose lap would I fall,
On a happy handsome hunk, smart and tall?
On a beautiful girl with a broken smile?
On a mom of two with a broken heart?
On a child who lost his Dad in a war,
On a teen living life, contemplating suicide?
On an old man who's seen success and falls?
Or somewhere far off, beautiful and calm?
As I continue my fall, a voice emerges from my heart,
With a whisper that reaches my mind,
'If I am to fall, it would be between it all,'
To uphold a few hands that have seen a fall.
—*Giridhar Karthik Jaded*

Note: Written on a certain flight back to Dallas, Texas, watching the sparkling light fest that the city looks like, at night.

A Late Bloomer

I am what they call a 'late bloomer,'
Like a sunflower from a May shower,
'Late' is often used for someone who's passed.
But 'Late' isn't a word in a dictionary of art,
It's a sad thing that some get known after their time,
As if their brilliance was there, just biding time,
I didn't just sit there and bide my time,
I was busy evolving on the outside and inside,
Every day that I lived was a lesson learned,
Which I now bring forth through what I write,
I had some demons that I had to kill,
Before I could start writing at will.
Now I am here, the Late Bloomer.
At times, I do get struck by mere wonder,
When I see a gem from a writer, singer, or a painter,
Making me wanna stay on much longer,
It's lovely to be part of this instant banter,
My Poems - the May flower, their influence – a Sunflower.

—*Giridhar Pramod Jaded*

Things I have planned

You said one day under a shade,
All our dreams shall be laid,
On a pedestal higher, made of gold,
With me and you and our hands to hold.

You said one day, on the road,
All the places we will roam,
Will be on a memory wall,
In a place we will call home.

You said one day on a high,
All the crazy things we shall try,
Shall make us laugh a while,
On days riding a rough tide.

You said one day on a walk,
All the good things I've planned,
Your hands shall always be in mine,
We would do it all with a smile.

—*Giridhar Shyam Jaded*

Masterstrokes

Who is it that I often see,
When you spend time with me?
Is it you in all your prime,
Or just a facade of what you hide?
Who is it that I often hear,
When we have a conversation?
Traversing places near and far,
From thoughts and inklings gone too far,
Is the voice yours or your hidden whisper?
Or is it my emptions running hither-thither?
What is it that I often feel?
When you hug or cuddle me,
Is it from an air of true love?
Or one more of your masterstrokes?
Do you make me a better me?
Or is this all a candid fallacy?
—*Giridhar Bapugowda Jaded*

Into the daylight

You left me in a place so empty,
I often find myself wanting aplenty,
With a sad-faced girl named Empathy.
We sit there, and we don't talk much, usually,
But every so often we look ahead and sulk.
There's an eerie feeling about the place, it irks.

It wipes off the positive vibes off my face.
The girl she's young, but no teeth, worn out grace,
She lost one tooth each time she realized,
The depths of her pain, from what had transpired.
I sit there because of the questions you left,
Was apathy the only thing in your farewell kit?
Empathy (my imaginary) and I, we started a weird journey,
One would ask a question painful and deep,
The other would have to answer and let it seep,
And the roles were reversed until the time,
Until Empathy and I walked into the daylight.

—*Giridhar Vijay Jaded*

Random Thoughts

Where do all the feelings go after a soul has departed the body? Do they cling to the soul as lessons learned? Or rather stay behind to see the bodily remains vanish? The feelings and emotions that fill our life's moments with intense sensations, they are an experience. The anguish you feel at something out of your control, the pain that you feel through hurtful words or actions, the love that you feel for someone far - all these are part of a process for the soul to develop into something better. Whatever the answers, this perspective helps to deal with feelings (of all kinds) better.

—Giridhar Adarsh Jaded

What You Once Said

If you sit somewhere and wonder,
Whether you ever cross my thoughts,
Let me tell you, you do.
I got a life to live with love too.

If you sit somewhere and wonder,
If I still feel your presence,
Let me tell you yes, I do.
But I got bigger things I like to do.

If you sit somewhere and wonder,
If I still admire and like you,
Let me tell you, I absolutely do.
I loved you, how can I not *like* you?

If you sit somewhere and wonder,
If we can be together, like before,
Let me tell you, we won't,
For it was you treating me like a don't.

—Giridhar Rajani Jaded

The threads you hold

I sometimes wonder why people are mean,
Is it because of what they have seen?
Or is it because of what they have been?
Or are they really angels in disguise?
Planted on Earth to give out advice,
Advice on how exactly NOT to be,
Advice on the ugly human frailties.

Are they mean from a severed thread?
Or is it from a struggle for daily bread?
Or is it just from a need to be plainly heard?
Or is it a heart filled with dead birds?
I wonder and wonder, but I don't get an answer,
And the mean ones seem to become meaner.

Being mean is an Art in a way,
To find new ways to push people away,
I hear what they say, and I make my point,
And I walk my way, wearing nothing but a smile,
When you are mean, the ropes that you hold on to,
Are threads concealed to give away, like they ought to.
—*Giridhar Hanumanthappa Jaded*

Story in the eyes

There's so much beauty in them eyes,
Often dwarfing other things that elegantly hide,
Behind the glistening H2O of the eyes,
Depicting if someone's living life or being alive.

If only, we all knew to read what's behind,
The eyes of the people we see in life.
But once in a while, the eyes do talk,
More so when butterflies flutter, when a heart walks.
But there are eyes not so good at playing,
The game of bait, switch, and hiding.
Some happy eyes sparkle clear and bright,
Some swollen eyes are from a ghastly night.
Some gloomy eyes have cried in the dark,
Some stony eyes play catch with demons in the park,
While some friendly eyes hold love in their hearts,
There are some who shine bright, but only in parts.
Every eye you look around, has a story to tell,
A pertinent question is whether you can read them well.

—*Giridhar Rachna Jaded*

In your thoughts

If you were a thought,
Something very light,
I would lift you up,
Hold you in my hands,
And take you on a ride,
To a place bereft of time.

Where you and me, my love,
Shall walk the sands,
Of Mt. Valentine.

I would sing a song,
From words - your offspring's,
I would make a tune,
From feeling your essence.
I drift along in your thought,
Missing you but finding your company,
In your thoughts.
—*Giridhar Pavitra Jaded*

Hey Mom, Good Morning

I sometimes think of what it was like,
When my Mom used to hold my hand.
When she used to hug me like I was blind,
Or when she yelled at me for being bad.
As these thoughts stay in a halo, I realize,
I must have sucked at the art to memorize.
Because a paltry few scenes come to my mind,
Scenes so murky, I now believe I was blind.
I try to imagine how her hug would feel,
Failing miserably as I can only squeal,
Sometimes I feel a gush of air, near my ear,
And I wonder if it's her, near her dear.
But then I wake up from those thoughts,
Gather myself and straddle on out,
Later that day at work, a phone rings;
Someone I knew picks up & says *"Hey Mom, Good Morning"*.
—*Giridhar Praful Jaded*

Legacies

A good day in my books,

Is something always in the works.

Sometimes I get it right,

Other times I mess it up.

An elevator door to hold,

A positive thought for one struggling to be bold,

A gentle act unnoticed done, not told,

At a place where it mattered the most,

And looking for ways for more,

An ignored feedback form at the store,

Or a notepad from a hotel I check out,

Words sometimes have the power,

To bring people closer than together,

Just like they can move people apart,

Even two souls who'd die if they part,

Words and actions and days lived are also a part,

Of the legacy we all leave behind.

—Giridhar Harsh Jaded

An emotional hook

Seven billion people on planet Earth,
Each with a story to be heard.
Some young, some in their prime,
Some ignorant, some biding their time.
Each of these billion people have a heart,
Filled with thousands of emotions inside,
I wonder how it would look,
If all emotions were to be hooked,
And brought to one common place,
In a round blurb that's transparent.
I shudder even at the thought,
Because emotions no matter how light,
Have the power to set it right,
Or cause doom in plain sight.
Will you help me with a hook?
To then stand along, admire, and just look.

—Giridhar Viaan Jaded

Not for fame

When your dreams are in sight,
Even if faint or far off sight,
Or hidden behind a cloud of mist,
Or teasing you, with scintillating twists,
Just know that it's alright,
For dreams are known to have a playful mind.

When your dreams sometimes go,
Into spaces you're not allowed,
And you tremble with the fright,
Of losing them from plain sight,
Just know that it's alright,
For you only need to hang on tight.

Those playful dreams, they're yours,
They ride alongside all your endeavors,
There's only one real winner in this game,
If you excel in your dream, not for money, nor for fame.
—*Giridhar Krustappa Jaded*

A vision unique

The people who stood tall, and left a legacy,
When you turn the pages of human history,
Were they made of blood and bones really?
Or did something else make them legendary?

Isn't it unfair to see only a select few,
Amongst billions of people that ever lived,
Leave a mark like no one else ever has?
Making us mortals sit back and clap,
Is it something they had deep in their hearts?
A raging fire to be the change, play a part?
Not joining a passing herd to say, *'Aye Sir,'*
Letting their mind and heart be heard, faced the ire,
The journey to being legendary isn't easy,
Ridicule and failures, a part of success, a path uneasy,
But a belief they had in their vision unique,
To be the change, leave behind lessons, and mystique.

—*Giridhar Deviramma Jaded*

Words with shapes

If the words we speak had a shape,
Ever wonder what'd they look like?
Would they be round or rather amoeba-like?
Or floating cloudlike shapes that would fill the skies?
Could they then be passed on as gifts?
Or would they be blown out of our reach?
Would all such gifts be in kind?
For we all tend to, often lose our minds.
Would the blue skies be filled with pleasant shapes?
From thoughts that found their way out those drapes,
Or would the words act as them mighty walls,
Like they do even now, without a mass or form?
The words in life even though invisible,
Hold the strength to make impossible possible,
If we find a way to apply a little filter,
Before the words eek out in ways helter-skelter,
And tame them words to act good often, then bad,
The shapes from words, certain to capture us, make us glad.

—*Giridhar Kashibai Jaded*

Learned to sail

Your words sometimes create a wave,
That lives inside of me for a while,
Taking me on a sail someplace far,
Through those seas rough, as well as mild.
Every time I sail, I look for you,
I see you letting go the anchor, letting me go.
Makes me wonder if you like me close,
Only when you feel lonely or cold,
I wonder so only for one reason,
Places you send me to, are filled with demons.
I sail to some places serene and beautiful,
But such visits are barely a handful,
If nothing, I have now learned to sail,
Bring on your hate waves, I still hate to fail.
The next time you release an anchor,
It won't be my boat for sure, end of chapter.
—Giridhar Manohar Jaded

Into the woods

As he whistled his way into the woods,
Looking around, taking in the sounds,
His mind was on the weekend ahead,
Smiling because he had no plans made.
He saw a hummingbird flutter away,
And a dumb looking owl, staring away,
As he walked on, he heard a twitch,
Stopped and wondered if its his mind playing tricks,
A gush of wind passed him, in that moment,
And he could hear his heart, feel its movement,
There was then a sudden ruffling of the leaves,
And the clouds darkened, suddenly looking mean,
The hopeful feeling from before, nowhere to be seen,
He then heard a wailing sound, from in between the greens,
As he went closer, his heart skipped a beat,
A Labrador pup stared at him, kissed him as a greet.
—*Giridhar Padma Jaded*

Nothing but Love

I play with your whiskers when I want,
I mess with your schedule when I want,
You keep wagging your tail and never flinch,
I wonder if you even feel a pinch.
Tell me now if you really do or don't,
I thought only in humans, was love lost.
That we alone were left to play our part,
Walking in sunshine or dancing in the dark,
With our conscience playing a heavy part,
Or banished from existence, inside colder hearts.

I wake you from your sleep when I want,
I ask for your cuddles when I want,
I wonder if there are times that I, fall short,
When you need me, and I am not around?
You fill my life with love, without a genetic bond,
Or a piece of paper saying we belong,
If you can read my mind, my best friend,
I have nothing but love for you till the end.

—*Giridhar Linganagouda Jaded*

Spaces meant to hide

What is it about creating Art?
Egging an artist to play his part,
Leaving behind pieces of their own,
Of their flesh, mind, and even their soul?
If Governments are the sentries of the world,
Artists I believe, are from the sanitary abode,
Trying to cleanse themselves and their minds,
In the process, leaving thoughtful Art behind.
Artists are like hardworking janitors in the dark,
Fearless unafraid to bring out a truth, even when stark,
Truth from spaces otherwise meant to hide,
From the rest of the world; not when an Artists glide,
Some make their mark while some don't,
Yet giving up for an Artist, is a big Won't,
In a league of its own, an Artist unwinds,
Known for the Art that is left behind.

—*Giridhar Geeta Jaded*

A window to the better

If every person on Earth picked up a pen,
And dwelled inside for what life has been,
And juggle with those thoughts left and right,
Until there was a lesson, in plain sight,
And penned it down as a thought,
A billion lessons, would it be worth it?

If a pen seems daunting, pick up a brush,
And mess up a canvas with that thought,
For there is Art in the act of expressing itself,
From those inner crevices, sadly, not dwelled.
Whatever your form, go find your own,
And create something you can call your own.
A candle burns in a room spreading light,
Unseen by most others, still shining bright.
Your Art might be lost in time, in a corner,
But it does open a window to feeling better.
—*Giridhar Vijayalakshmi Jaded*

Sing along

A denim jacket for the winter,
A leather one for the summer,
Something about carrying a swagger,
Makes me wanna keep looking dapper.
A bunch of colognes to choose from,
A few dollar bills in my possession,
For someone in need at a streetlight,
I try to keep things rather light.
A torn shoe that I wear once a while,
To remind myself of the rough slides,
That I sailed through feeling alright,
With a clear vision always in sight.
A few pages of what I wrote,
Back in my teens, when I was on a stroll,
Makes me smile in a moment of innocence,
For even back then, Art in me had its essence,
Some things we carry, carry us along,
Making us who we are, why not just sing along?
—*Giridhar Ashok Jaded*

Beauty called Meditation

Once in a while, if not daily,
We should try to see beauty,
With eyes closed, not open,
As it is in the darkness that beauty blossoms.
Spend a moment of time,
Doing nothing but feeling alive,
It takes something to do nothing,
And to just continue breathing.
To just be and feeling one's presence,
The sounds, the breath and its essence.
If a crowded mind is your excuse,
My friend - you shall never have a recluse.
If you can't shoo away the thoughts,
There are guided meditation apps,
Comfort is from doing uncomfortable things,
Act different, for we can, as human beings.
—*Giridhar Ramanagouda Jaded*

Strangers called words

Is it just me or do you feel this too?
For sometimes the very words I use,
Time and again, seem like strangers.
Making me wonder if I need better inner glasses.
Even with my eyes closed, when I think,
About the word, it nonchalantly winks,
I consider myself well-read, but this gives me the creeps,
For it's the mysterious things, that usually run deep.
I write the words down and stare on,
The meaning is quite clear; then what's going on?
I dive deeper, peeling off the layers,
In search of those elusive answers,
That's when it strikes me with a jolt,
Words also have a duty, truth be told,
It's what the words felt or made someone feel,
The matters in the end, when looked from an even keel.

—*Giridhar Anysuya Jaded*

The Valentines Mug

The mug that I gave you on Valentines,
After you said 'Yes' to being mine,
With a pic of me and you that looked pristine.
It's a sign of those wonderful times.
It broke by accident, I don't know how,
A moment of recklessness cost me, and how.
Now, when I look at the broken pieces,
I could relive that accident, even write a thesis,
On how not to break into pieces, a souvenir of Love,
Of how not to be careless, when on the move.
I turn, think and start to curse gravity instead,
A part of me knows its not right, plainly said.
Jokes apart, I've saved the pieces for a purpose,
To try and resurrect them as one, from pieces.
It won't be easy, there shall be spaces,
Which I shall fill with pictures of places,
That we visited once and had a blast,
I want this feeling to forever last.
—*Giridhar Subhash Jaded*

Never ever

To all the mean people in my life,
Whom I admire in a different light,
As people caught up in life's haze,
Driven by greed, envy, hatred, caught in a maze,
I admire you for you show me how not to be,
I stay clear, and I walk down my alley.
I smile at you for I know you have a battle to win,
To make believe that kindness is not a sin.
It is in fact, a beautiful way of plain living,
A fulfilling way of being caring and giving.
While you battle it out, I keep my kindness alive,
Just for a while and I continue my ride.
From where you are now, you won't understand,
As your feet are underground, deep in quick sands.
I'm sorry I'm not gonna wait for you,
But I ain't got the time to sit, notice and to hate you,
Go find your way or be stuck where you are,
Either we meet on my road, or never ever.
—Giridhar Myna Jaded

Till the end of time

My Dad was a man of a few words,
But he knew how to pick on the chords,
Chords that ring in my ears even today,
As guiding lights showing me the way.
He spoke less but his actions, were vibrant,
Creating ripples that touched lives, of patients.
My Mom was someone who felt a lot,
Seeing others entrapped in life's riot.
She had a say in everything, often uninvited,
Most called her nosy, she was unperturbed.
The seeds of wanting to be good to all,
I guess they were planted by Dad and Mom,
Of all the lessons I learned in books,
Or from loitering around life, chasing hooks,
The lessons they taught in very little time,
Shall stay with me till the end of time.

—*Giridhar Vasundhara Jaded*

Out the abyss

Mirror, mirror on the wall,
Can you somehow stop my fall?
Into an abyss dark and long,
And catch me before I'm gone?
Mirror, mirror on the wall,
Where have all the smiles gone?
I see a shadow lurking behind,
It's not mine but they look alike.
Mirror, mirror on the wall,
Where are all the lovely times,
When I romanced you all the while?
I have time now but lost my vibe.
Mirror, mirror on the wall,
Do you have a potion nice and small?
That can help me learn to fly,
To jump out the abyss, into the sky?

—*Giridhar Shrikant Jaded*

Mostly you, and us

A painting class during school,
Is when I really understood,
That Art does favors to some,
And I wasn't one of them.

But when I look at you, my love,
I see a beautiful sky so blue,
A rainbow too lovely to be true,
A canvas of colors fresh and new.
Before I know it, there I am,
The dreamy painter with a brush,
Trying to paint a picture of you,
In shades of pink, yellow, orange, and blue.
I hold the brush like a pro,
Using it in ways never ever known,
But I shall try to paint that canvas,
And fill it with beautiful parts of mostly you, and us.

—*Giridhar Pavan Jaded*

Random Thoughts

A small fish – underdeveloped and easy prey in an ocean full of predators – finds its survival trick, it's hunger to live, in a poisonous creature with tentacles. It swims alongside the protector, careful every second to not come in contact with the tentacles. A single brush with her could summon the demon called Death. This weird partnership is for three months, after which it's time for another perfectly poisonous host. Pushed to their limits, animals don't have a choice but to fight or die. If we're so intelligent, why do humans let other humans suffer in hunger, violence, and ignorance?

—Giridhar Apoorva Jaded

Happy Women's day

What was the master plan?
When men and women were created differently?
Like they say, there's always a reason,
If we look beyond what's real.
Men are made tough on the outside,
Women, a factory of strength on the inside.
A factory that mass produces on assembly lines,
Leaving products as good deeds, most of the times.
A man's heart beats mostly on instinct,
A woman's heart beats with a meaningful precinct,
If men had go through half of what women do,
We wouldn't have men at all, truth be told.
Here's a salute for being who you are,
The women who help take the world further and far.

—Giridhar Prashanth Jaded

Battle for lives

What does it take for someone to enlist?
Into a selfless national service,
And leave behind every other need,
For the safety of the regular breed?
Regular because we are driven by needs,
While a soldier is driven by heart and deeds.
Doesn't a soldier have a heart?
Ripe with feelings like most of us?
They do, but the feelings are wrapped,
Neatly packed and put aside.
When the time comes to do it right,
A soldier fights for us with all his might.
It's hard to feel what a soldier does,
Our battles with life, versus their battle for lives.
If not for men in duty, what would we do?
Continue living life, like we always do?
—*Giridhar Madhura Jaded*

Bring it on

Bring on your shades of judgment,
Bring on your air of misplaced arrogance,
Bring on your bag of curse words,
Bring on your rants and your swords,
Saddle on your backpack filled with hate,
Write down all your rants, please add dates,
Bring on your sea of misunderstandings,
Bring on your pot of belittling things,
Bring on your niche in playing games,
Bring on your gait in calling names,
Bring along your dark clouds of ignorance.
Dress up your best, wear your acting skins,
For my eyes can see through sometimes.
Bring it on, I have crossed a few turbulent times,
I have an answer to all your fallacies,
I have a solution to all your fantasies,
I have built a mindful haven of my own,
Where vibes like yours are beaten up and thrown.

—Giridhar Mridula Jaded

Save our Oceans

While we lay awake, or when we sleep,
While our days beckon, and nights are deep,
With things not worthy to even repent,
There's another world, existing mostly in silence,
Under a carpet of water spread for miles,
A blue carpet over 70% of planet Earth,
A sea of abundance, for what its worth.
Oceans make us feel like minions,
As mortals caught up fighting oblivion.
A sunny day at the beach, and pictures to take,
To then call it a day, after memories have been made.
But why spill your trash onto beaches or the oceans,
To mess up the beautiful, do some minds even reason?
Also spare a thought for what's inside,
A harmony of life lives beneath, it resides,
Harmony exists even between prey and predators,
And beauty unseen to the naked eye, and intruders,
We won't survive long without our oceans,
I guess it's time to be responsible humans.

—*Giridhar Kiran Jaded*

Miss you

I notice a strand of your hair on my bed,
A shiny black one that you had shed,
While you lay next to me and smiled,
It's been a month; it's been a while.
It takes me back to a beautiful time,
When I was yours, and you were mine.
I pick up the strand and set it aside,
Until we meet again, the next time.
I could throw it away, but I really can't,
Your presence in any form is all I want.
Your scent is dead, but my mind is alive,
I close my eyes, relive and feel alive.
We live apart, but our hearts are twined,
In beautiful knots, permanently joined.
Until next time we meet again,
You are here with me and in my mind.

—Giridhar Tejraj Jaded

A costly toss

On a sunny day under a beautiful blue sky,
Riding on waves over the deep blue sights,
If heaven was on Earth, it was right here,
When a family of five set out on a sail.
A distressed-looking Dad, a chore-less Mom,
A daughter aged eight, son ten, toddler at one,
The breeze was beautiful, the tides playful,
Seemed a perfect place to be in June.
Mom was over-relaxed and forgot to pack,
A bag of fruits or a healthy snack.
Hunger doesn't wait, it actually baits,
Savior – a plastic filled vending machine, it awaits,
They had their fill and nonchalantly spilled,
The colorful venom into the blue ocean.
The vacation's over, pictures uploaded,
Lives perish – unwillingly, Thanks to your plastic gift.
—*Giridhar Naveen Jaded*

A Song in my mind

I hum to a song in my mind,
It's silent yet feels soothing and kind,
It fills me up with unending hope,
Coercing me into never say 'Nope.'

I hum to a song in my mind,
It feels present yet from the past,
It fills me up with a passion unknown,
To try and be myself more often, on my own.

I hum to a song in my mind,
The beats they make me go wild,
It fills me up with unending energy,
Drifting my mind and body into a blissful synergy.

I hum to a song in my mind,
Close my eyes, listen deep feeling blind,
It pushes me to be a better me,
It's not rock, pop, jazz, nor a lullaby.

—*Giridhar Nitin Jaded*

Taken for a ride

I let you be by my side,
To be taken for a ride,
I let you dwell inside of me,
To be left feeling empty.
I let you see my soul,
To now find a gaping hole.
I let you ride my highs,
To be left digging burrows.
I let you be yourself,
And now I am lost myself.
I let you wet your beak,
To be left sulking and weak.
I let you in, deep inside,
To be walked on, shoved aside.
But I didn't let you own me,
I'm on my way to being me.
—*Giridhar Nandan Jaded*

Broken wings

A child who is supposed to jump in joy,
Sulks in a corner, amidst abandoned toys.
Hidden from sight from adults alike,
Who seem too caught up, in unraveling life,
A child who has forgotten to smile,
Walks in parties, almost zombie like,
For adults around are too lost,
For a future bright or in their pasts.
A child who knows to hide his scars,
Under the soft branded tees Dad brought,
Learns to live most of life being lost,
Without even knowing that one's even lost.
Raising a child is a sacred Art,
Where parents ought to play their vital part.
Broken wings – the worst societal handicap,
Parenting in a way shapes our future and that's a fact.
—*Giridhar Deepthi Jaded*

Juggling life

Sometimes I feel as if I have been dropped off,
From an emotional train that hopped off,
Dropped in a secluded place strange and unknown,
Maybe to find some answers on my own.
I stand there and wave a goodbye,
A *'see you later'* it is, for later to return,
I watch the emotions leave me alone,
Even if for a moment, just a few moments on my own,
I stand there, shivering in the cold,
A voice in me whispers 'Be fucking bold.'
I've trained my thoughts to walk apart,
From feelings for a while, because they hurt.
I spend some time being myself,
And I hear a whistle, to then see an incoming train,
And I hop on, ready to juggle with life again.
—*Giridhar Abhishek Jaded*

Time capsule

If our hearts had a time capsule,
With a button to turn the tides on time,
And take us to those very memories,
From our past, that bring about a smile,
How happier would the world be?
A reverse flying plane, a reality?
Seeing people pack a little and scurry,
To their pasts, as presents were tricky.
What would the future look like?
If everyone lived back in their pasts?
What would the children of tomorrow learn?
That it's alright to give in to fears?
There's a reason no such button exists,
For time never halts, never retreats.
There's a choice for each of us to make,
To live in our pasts or to look ahead.
—*Giridhar Shwetha Jaded*

Gazing in the dark

Some nights I go to bed early,
To a place of intrigue and mystery,
With shining curtains on the walls,
Glistening even in the deathly dark,
A faint light emanating from my heart,
Which has a little bit of a fight left.
I can't sleep early, but I can be,
Gazing in the dark 'till eternity,
And feel my thoughts consume me,
Until they become a soothing lullaby.
Some nights, thoughts are a paltry few,
While sometimes they fill the room,
I imagine shiny stars and alleys dark,
Beautiful sometimes, others stark.
It's a ritual that doesn't always work,
Yet a sumptuous thought feast makes it worth.

—Giridhar Avinash Jaded

I tried

If it were really up to me,
I would never let you turn,
Into this person you have become,
I thought you were sensible.
The tantrums you blindly threw,
Had my heart bleeding blue,
From the blood that was bright red,
Rotten in time into hues of blue,
I went into a zone unknown,
Away from the world, withdrawn,
Maybe you had fully drawn,
Water from the well of my love,
And saw me never go dry,
No matter how hard you tried,
I am glad all this isn't on me,
Your thoughts shall soon be history.
—*Giridhar Pratik Jaded*

What Did I Do?

Did I open the gate, let you in by mistake?
Or did life have this cruel lesson to teach?
For I fail to climb the walls and breach,
This question eating me like a leech.
Maybe it was me who went overboard,
Believing every word that you ever spoke,
And getting caught up in this maze,
To which only you had the master keys.
Did I get so blinded by the lights of love?
That I unlearned everything I once knew,
About predators that know just of prey,
On souls wanting love that dutifully pray.
You are a player of a different league,
Perfecting the art of laying a siege,
Unto innocent hearts that easily bleed,
I am out, Good luck to you chasing your needs.

—*Giridhar Karthik Jaded*

An unimaginable nightmare

What if one day, out of the worldly blue,
An unimaginable nightmare did come true,
That humans were no longer the only ones on Earth,
With the ability to contemplate, to make it worth.
Dominance has become part of our genes,
From centuries of sustained abuse and silent memes,
Between humans and all the lives around,
Crushing the weaker ones with our greed alone,
Masked by the shield of intelligence,
Making the most insane of decisions,
What would all the animals say first?
Raging in anger, filled with bloodthirst.
If nature has given us an ability to think,
Why do we push others to the brink?
If the tides turn one day even a tad bit,
Won't be much left of us to act, or to think.
—*Giridhar Rashmi Jaded*

Board that flight

Which way are you headed now?
Do you mind if I come along?
I think I have lost my way out here,
All I want is to be somewhere.
Some place where I can be myself,
Not just another book on the shelf,
That catches dust, never gets read,
For I got stories wanting to be heard.
Will you take me to a place not far?
Where I can cleanse away my scars,
Or maybe just lighten them up a tad bit,
For I am a love song, waiting to be a hit.
If you ain't got a seat, let me know,
I booked a one-way ticket long ago.
Maybe it's time to board that flight,
And see if I end up seeing the light.
—*Giridhar Preethi Jaded*

Being Kind

Poignant faces, with hidden lines,
From life, not from biding time.
Hidden because of lines so dark,
Nightmares guaranteed; what a sight.
Sullen faces, with angst inside,
From life and missed chances alike.
Anger that burns, curdling the blood,
A beautiful tree reduced to a log.
Anxious faces, wrinkled and covered,
In cosmetics of the finest kind,
Hiding fears, and demons alike,
Afraid to switch off lights at night.
Face, a mere reflection of a state of mind,
Either live dying, caught up in the grind,
Or smile a lot, reasons yours to find.
If nothing works, solace is in being kind.
—*Giridhar Kashi Nath Jaded*

Accidents

Spare a thought for those who perished,
In a plane crash recent, taken by surprise.
Spare a thought for the ones that died,
And for the ones that they left behind.
What is it like to suddenly not have?
Someone with whom you share your blood,
or someone whom you've loved?
What is it like to suddenly vanish and die?
Without a farewell, or a proper goodbye?
There's a rage that burns inside like fire,
Trying to find someone to blame for the misfire.
It takes a while for realization to dawn,
That life sometimes is a knight and we the pawns.
I lost someone like that when I was a child,
With questions in my mind, unanswered still.
What would I look like from up above?
Am I a story to Love or a sorry picture, with a red rose?

—*Giridhar Kiran Jaded*

Technology —The boon & the doom

An Xbox game in the backpack,
A VR as a jewel flaunted with pride,
A curved television to brag about,
A personal iPad for homework,
A social game played online,
An online persona growing with time,
An inquisitive mind filled with thoughts,
Forcibly on topics around gadgets.
What we see a lot, become our thoughts,
Are the children of today bright or lost?
Not knowing what it's like to play,
Not with toys but with nature and clay.
Not knowing what it's like to just play,
Without toys, finding games in company.
Technology is a boon as well as a doom,
A cautious mix better if perfected soon.

—Giridhar Kotish Jaded

Strangers in the crowd

Walking in these crowded streets,
Where there's plenty to see and eat,
I often bump into a stranger or two,
Who seem to be stranded in glue,
They gaze around, standing alone,
Like a lost compass on a tailspin.
Looking here and there as if to think,
'Which way is the world's brink?'
If I have the time, I people watch,
People like these are my golden catch.
It's fun to sometimes stand and observe,
Moments that even strangers offer.
Lost in my thoughts, I stand there,
Regain my senses, and he's not there,
I lost the stranger, when in thought,
Or my thoughts were the ones lost?
—Giridhar Aanshi Jaded

Die another day

I would live to die another day,
For I have a lot more left to say.
Death now would be a bad twist,
I haven't even started with the gist.
The words inside me are crazy,
Can't see my mind being lazy.
Often sending me into a frenzy,
Or luring me into a sweet symphony.
What I say might make sense,
Or be dispelled, as mere nonsense,
But having let out these words,
I feel lighter in my second world.
If anything, I would love to see,
A smile here, a nod there,
A sigh here, a release elsewhere.
Words and thoughts are beautiful parts, I want to share.
—Giridhar Ananya Jaded

Lost in your eyes

Her tresses flutter like satin in the wind.
Her lips quiver like shaken red wine,
Her breath sends a chill down my spine.
Boy, does she know to take me on a ride.
Her touch made me wanna be in those skies,
She makes me forget I am inherently shy.
Her words make their home inside of me,
Fueled by admiration, her words are now a colony.
Her hug makes the man inside of me melt,
Struggling to put to words what I have felt.
There's a peace unlike any other,
When I am lost looking into her eyes, amidst the glitter.
The world would a new meaning for her,
If only I had the gumption now, to walk up to her,
And to whisper in her ears or to boldly tell her,
That beauty is alright, it does create a flutter,
But would you tell me, what else is the matter?
For there's a heart inside that keeps a counter,
Of the games being played, it doesn't stutter,
Why, are you then seen running helter-skelter?

—*Giridhar Amit Jaded*

A place called time

In a place called time,
Far away from land,
There shall be a shiny light,
That most have never seen.
I shall wait over there,
For you to come over,
And when you are with me,
Is when I shall smile with glee.
Time freezes in a place so far,
Hunger vanishes, fed by love.
And you, my Dear, whom I crave,
Shall hold my hands in a cave.
A song, we shall sing along,
Days beautiful, nights so long.
In a place called Time,
I'll be yours, and you will be mine.
—*Giridhar Deepak Jaded*

A Thank You, not said

A drive to a restaurant on a Sunday,
Started feeling like a chore – mundane,
For a simple fact he tried to explain,
Sprayed their tempers in all ways.
He wondered in silence on the drive,
What would have happened if he'd replaced words with a smile,
A smile of admiration towards her,
The way she'd dressed – a real stunner.
But he'd let it pass for a stupid thought,
That he knew, would foster conflict, then on out,
The first few minutes spent in silence,
Orders were placed, followed by silence.
Her favorite food arrived, tasting delicious,
A faint blush hidden beneath the eyelashes.
Walked out holding hands, anger gone,
Without thanking the chef for a job well done.
—*Giridhar Prashanth Jaded*

A Pizza Delivery Gone Wrong

On a certain wound up Friday night,
When I was feeling lazy and uptight,
I heard a grumble deep inside,
Hunger pangs on the prowl alright.
I pick up the phone, place an order,
Before I heard my belly moan grow into a thunder.
I ignored the sounds, lost in thought,
Yet once in a while, I felt them all on out.
An hour later, still no food in sight,
A canceled order – sorrier became my plight.
Picked up the phone, asked on away,
Didn't help in keeping my hunger at bay,
Then a fleeting thought struck my mind,
I can order again – a different place, money makes people kind,
But what if I was a homeless man, perched outside,
Hungry from days, waiting for bread, waiting for the kind.
—*Giridhar Krishna Jaded*

The unknown, untold

If I had seen the unknown,
Or known the unseen,
What would my thoughts be?
Or would there be any?

If I had felt the warmth,
Or warmed up my feelings,
Where would my mind be?
Probably found or lost in obscurity.

If I had tasted the tasteless,
Or lost my sense of taste,
What would my body say?
'Let's face it come what may?'

If I didn't make any sense,
That's how this was meant,
A thought or two evoked,
A mystery poem – as well can provoke.
—*Giridhar Sudha Jaded*

A difference, in time

What makes some people go deep,
Into places that give us the creeps,
With a common goal, they set out,
On a conquest that us ordinary cannot.
Are there fears that reside in them?
Or is there a calm totally unseen,
By us, the regular people in life,
That keeps their flames from flickering.
To keep their comforts aside and to live a life,
Of battling the elements, rough seas to ride.
For they have a passion hard to imagine,
To live a life to make a difference, in time.
It's not easy to tread such paths,
Where discomfort reins the horses, in every walk,
For a journey for others, through treacherous mountains.
In today's self-centered world, akin to feeding snakes to falcons?
—*Giridhar Shobha Jaded*

A bucket full of dreams

Those silent looks that you send my way,
Can you tell me what do they even mean?
Do they have something sweet to say?
Or a silent way of telling me to keep away?

Those hidden smiles you send my way,
Do they hide words forbidden to be said?
Or are there demons from the past wanting to be laid,
To rest, and wanting to find newer ways?

Those blank stares that you send my way,
That look to me like an innocent cry for help,
Tell me are my assumptions misplaced?
For all I seek is them worries being frayed.

The questions that you send my way,
Will they have answers one day?
Silence is bliss, but oh it can also kill,
I have a dream bucket waiting to be filled.

—Giridhar Shilpa Jaded

Something to do

Monday is the start of a calendar week,
Most of us get up and plan our commute,
Doesn't help seeing a few online posts,
All ruing about nothing but Monday blues.
A sad emoji or a pup curled up in bed,
Making us want to be in that place instead.
For a moment imagine yourself like that,
Without anything to do, for about a month.

On a Monday later when you have rested,
Lazed around, felt like a king or a queen, having feasted,
You will then mot notice a sleeping pup,
But rather a success story from someone, lost in work.
On the same social media that had made,
You cringe a month ago, feeling betrayed.
And you yearn for something to do,
We humans weren't meant to sit and sulk it through.

—*Giridhar Kittu (Pramod) Jaded*

Who painted Monday blue?

Who has painted Mondays blue?
Was it nature, or someone without a clue,
Or someone who hated life on a schedule?
Oftentimes one says, and the rest of us fall through.
Is it the nature of work that you hate?
Or the feeling of being controlled, not by fate?
If you don't have a choice, then it's fate,
But if you do, you have yourself to blame.
Some work by choice, some in a vice,
Everyone wants to be in a place, very nice.
If not for work, what else would you do?
Money and luxury would not feed your soul.
Change the train or fall into line,
Or you're blocking someone awaiting their time,
Most, if not all, are a product of our choices,
All days can be beautiful, as a whole, not in traces.

—Giridhar Sunil Jaded

Humans and the brilliance

Truth be told, humans are brilliant,

If we look at inventions, magnificent.

The discoveries both new and ancient

Or for traits unworldly and valiant.

Truth be told, humans have the might;

To solve mysteries, easy and insurmountable alike.

From conquering diseases rabid,

To turning dreams – like flying – into a habit.

Truth be told, humans are well equipped,

To overcome fears and fight resistance,

For intellect works on both sides,

To be washed away in tides or nailing right the rides.

Truth be told, humans have the strength,

To move mountains on the outside, and inside.

For when intellect is directed to being kind,

The world looks beautiful, and one of a kind.

—*Giridhar Mamatha Jaded*

In Love with you

You take me to horizons unknown,
Where smiles glow brighter than the sun,
Where beauty is in every grain of sand,
Otherwise sane, you just blow my mind.
I feel a warmth, not from the sunlight,
But from butterflies dancing in twilight.
Deep inside me, they burst out in joy,
An outburst of colors, beauty for the eyes.
You cast a spell I have never known,
Many tricks I mastered, but never this one.
To call it a trick would be a shame,
A smile is all I want when I call your name.
You send me flying high into the skies,
Far away from creed, greed, and the lies.
You are absolutely one, one of a kind,
In love with you, oh my beautiful mind.

—Giridhar Suresh Jaded

If I were a Bird

If I were a bird, would I be in a flock,
Or a loner far away on a rock?
Would I fly with them all, or alone?
Flapping my wings in solace, as one?

If I were a bird, how would I fly,
Across the oceans or into the sky?
Would I be in the comfort of others,
Or alone somewhere fixing feathers?

If I were a bird, which way would I fly,
Where most do, or my own sacred mile?
Would I be like a leaf blown in the wind,
Or a peach hanging against mighty winds?

If I was a bird, how would I live and die,
A silent exit or a violent outcry?
If I have wings, I am meant to fly,
Came in an egg, but I'll die in the skies.

—Giridhar Shashan Jaded

Letters not posted

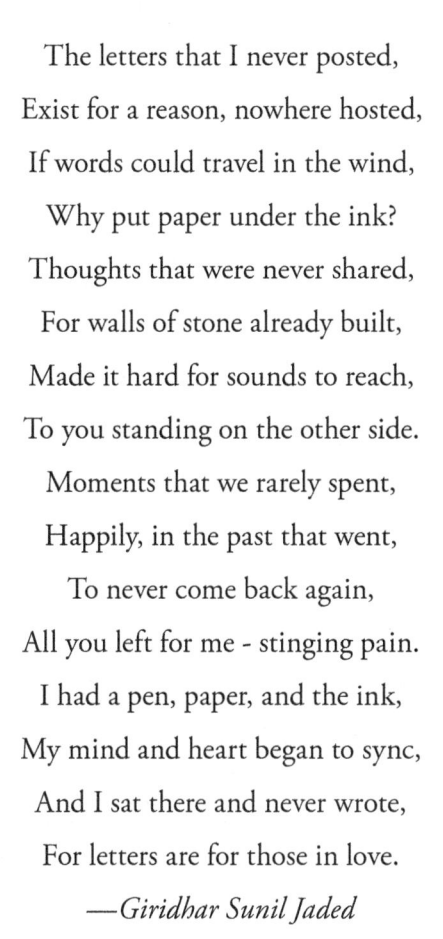

The letters that I never posted,
Exist for a reason, nowhere hosted,
If words could travel in the wind,
Why put paper under the ink?
Thoughts that were never shared,
For walls of stone already built,
Made it hard for sounds to reach,
To you standing on the other side.
Moments that we rarely spent,
Happily, in the past that went,
To never come back again,
All you left for me - stinging pain.
I had a pen, paper, and the ink,
My mind and heart began to sync,
And I sat there and never wrote,
For letters are for those in love.
—*Giridhar Sunil Jaded*

Note: Broken word poetry where the sentences do not fit in yet pitch in.

Before my fall

If there's a fire somewhere in me,
I find myself looking for a matchstick,
To light it up and set it ablaze,
And spread light to uncover the maze.
If there's a dream somewhere in me,
I find myself randomly distracted, repeatedly,
By side thoughts that pull me away,
Trying to send me reeling, ashtray.
If there's a sea of emotions in me,
I keep looking for outlets to let them free,
For what if I can feel but not heal,
Someone in need or facing the heat?
If there's a sense of good in me,
I am on the lookout for opportunities,
To make a difference big or small,
To have eased some pain before my fall.
—*Giridhar Sharath Jaded*

A rainbow called Life

At times I see life like a rainbow,
Filled with colors grim and cheerful,
And I see phases with clarity,
Just like a rainbow has disparity.
There's a meeting of colors faint,
When violet meets with indigo,
Or when green meets yellow,
There's a phenomenon on a flow.
What I feel and what I go through,
Are nothing but a pass though,
From being lesser to being more,
All ways to strengthen my core.
My life is my canvas, I hold the brush,
My victory to paint or my loss,
A picture gloomy or beautiful.
I choose the latter and walk on, forever hopeful.
—*Giridhar Rakesh Jaded*

Love isn't Life

If Love between a couple could feed the hungry lives,
Maybe no one would have ever died,
Starving for a meal, searching in dread,
For a piece of food; not any other greed.
If love could bring about a change,
So potent it could transform lives,
With money in bank and poverty aside,
The world would be a great journey to glide.
Truth is, love can fill the air, with a feeling fair,
Or bail out a thirsty heart caught in despair,
But it can't move the ugly boulders,
If we can't carry the needy on our shoulders.
Love is a need, but compassion a deed,
A mix of which is omnipotent indeed,
Look around and when you see someone in need,
Do your bit in planting a kindness seed.

—*Giridhar Praveen Jaded*

Note: The Love being referred to here is a rivulet of Love between consenting adults, not the bigger all-encompassing feeling of Love.

Daily life

The so-called irritants of daily life,
Like annoying people, and unfinished tasks,
Are nothing but a state of our minds.
More we let them seep, mightier the winds,
That sway us away from our goals,
Drifting us wayward into rougher shores.
The so-called worries in daily life,
From an unpaid bill or vacations missed,
Are also nothing but a play in our minds,
Shooed away only through our actions in kind.
There's a science in battling worries;
It starts off when you secretly list them down,
And beating them up one by one, in time,
Helps to transfer your worries of mind,
Onto a paper ever so accepting and kind,
To take the burden off your mind.
—*Giridhar Vishal Jaded*

Food for thought.: There's a term for the process of giving form to pending irritants, on paper.

A place named serenity

Is there a place named Serenity?
Where we could travel frequently?
Not with bags and clothing alike,
But via a route inside the mind.
How beautiful would it really be?
To get away from life's melancholy,
To put a hold on time for a while,
And drift aimlessly in a calm.
To stow away the niggles of life,
Feeling one's existence for a while.
Even if it doesn't bring about a smile,
A visit like that would be sublime.
A trip like this is in our hands,
Meditation indeed has a magic wand.
Or dispel in an Art that makes your heart and mind travel,
Where virtues come and make home, and mysteries unravel.

—Giridhar Ravi Jaded

A probe – deeper

Who am I to judge you,
And who are you to judge me?
Opinions of yours rather be,
Tucked aside or shoved inside.
I shall kill my own little minions,
Cute looking beastly opinions,
And then the world will be,
Altogether a better place to be.
If life is an experience,
I would rather experience,
Then dishing out justifications,
To your unwelcome opinions.
I'd rather spend my time,
Unraveling my mysteries inside,
For the answers are always better,
When the probing is deeper.
—*Giridhar Gokul Jaded*

Angel from the skies

If I was a symphony,
Would you be my melody?
If I was a century,
Would you be my history?
If I was a memory,
Would you be my sanity?
If I was a mystery,
Would you be my only key?
If I were a treachery,
Would you be my alibi?
If I lived in chastity,
Would you be my vanity?
If I lived in Italy,
Would you be my Sicily?
If I was a dynasty,
Would you be my hierarchy?
If I was at the rock bottom,
Would you still be my underground?
If my heart were bereft of spiteful lies,
Would you be my angel from the skies?
—*Giridhar Prashanth Jaded*

Remnants of our pasts

If there was an eraser ever made,

That could wipe off all the pain,

I wonder what it would then cost,

To bring back souls that are lost.

Would it erase all those scars?

Or would it leave behind faint little marks,

Giving aching hearts a clean slate?

Rekindling hope to change fate.

Would it wipe out everything clean,

Even the blissful moments felt and seen?

Or would it wipe the memory blank,

For a new beginning from the start?

Would you buy an eraser like that?

Or live life, accepting the facts?

We're remnants of what we've gone through,

Every moment a new start – only if we want to.

—Giridhar Kiran Jaded

I called It a day

You told me that you would never run away;

My feelings - the last game that you would play.

You told me you will never shy away,

From me, my advances, or my anxious play.

You told me you will never smile that way,

When I am broken and sulking my day away.

You told me that you would never move away,

Let alone spend a moment looking away.

You gave me hope the carpe diem way,

You made me live life in MY own way.

Where are you now, what made you run away?

What made our love to just shy away?

I'm done looking for answers – I've called it a day;

Won't hear you even if you had a million words to say.

—Giridhar Sandeep Jaded

Some place, free

Will you lead me to place?
Careful not to leave a trace,
That we were even there?
Rain or shine, I don't care.
A place where there is time,
And no sense of yours or mine.
A place so beautiful indeed,
What else do we really need?
We shall bask in the pain,
Or dance in the spring rains,
A freedom, one of a kind,
Careless souls glad to be freed.
If you find a trail to that place,
Leading through this worldly maze,
Holler at me, I shall race,
Fighting through the blinding haze.
Once there, together we shall see,
Beauty from the forests and the seas,
A peace unknown in being free,
Only if our fickle minds are free.
—*Giridhar Vinayak Jaded*

Unraveling Depression

What is depression anyway?
At best, fallacies of mind at play.
What's in the mind anyway?
Thoughts that simmer and sway.
What does simmer anyway?
Something inside wanting to change.
What's inside us anyway?
Darkness or light leading the way.
What's darkness anyway?
An absence of light in a way.
What lights up your gloomy days?
An answer to that is the way.
Depression is a game in the mind,
Twisting your soul into a spiral bind,
Only if you are ever so kind,
To let it grow and raise its hood, behind,
There's always a choice, anyway,
To be lost, or to find your own way.
—*Giridhar Ramakrishna Jaded*

Inside the mind of a newborn

The feeble sounds I heard earlier,
Are now clearer and louder.
I still see just red in my sight, but it's brighter,
I can't wait to open my eyes and discover life's banter.
I am amazed at the sounds I can make,
Learning tricks every waking moment like a piece of cake.
I now feel warmth, I also feel cold,
I feel myself changing as a whole.
I make sounds when hungry, cranky, or naughty,
There's so much to learn – am I late to the party?
I hear laughter, I hear happy cries,
Some even amuse me with sounds and whistles.
I finally open my eyes, and I see life,
So colorful, so vibrant, filled with smiles.
I observe everything and try to make sense,
But there's so much attention always on me,
That I wonder if I should learn false pretense,
To act as sleeping while my mind processes inside – wide awake.

—*Giridhar Daniel Jaded*

A Blissful Evening

Blissful evenings like this were a rare sight,
With the sun shining and the rays light.
Jamie and Landon walked the park hand in hand,
It was a lawn, but beneath their feet they felt the sand.
The breeze sounded to them like ocean waves,
And miles ahead – amidst picturesque beauty – the human caves.
These moments of togetherness for them were eternal bliss,
In lonely moments, there should be feelings too strong to miss.
Jamie was more than the light in Landon's eyes,
She was the vision and the future – always having a space in his heart.
Landon had known only to love,
Men like him were an enigma to see through.
They had been together lesser than they wished,
But boy those moments they had really lived!
They knew no boundaries - they were plainly in love,
Souls were united - the bodies just played along.
Their moments were not counted by the clock,
But by the memories at each opportunity that gave a knock.
The sun slowly started to bid his farewell,
The warmth from his rays started to dispel.
A chill went down Jamie's spine, stinging her like a ray,
She was normal now – madness out the door – what had happened today?
It seemed so beautiful, yet what was it?
Hallucinations for Jamie were now a thing of the past.

Earlier as their shoulders had brushed,
She noticed a pink blush on his cheeks had formed,
And she ignored a certain difference in the texture of his hands,
But was there more that transpired in these imaginary sands?
In a snap, the logical part of her brain came back from its trip,
It was 2:00 a.m. now, and she stood in her lawn, hand on hip.
When she felt something on her hand, Jamie glanced down,
Found the scar from his nails as he'd fought not to drown.
Jamie couldn't move a muscle, nor shed a tear,
Landon was alive in her heart but had been dead for a year.

—Giridhar Vikas Jaded

Note: Jamie and Landon are names from the movie "A Walk to Remember" which is a beautiful rendition on Love.

I Love You, Mom

A smile I saw on your glowing face,
When you first realized the signs.
Two hearts inside, you began to pace,
A soul inside of you made you feel gentle pains.
I was really small, I was scared a lot,
To open my eyes in a world I wasn't a part of.
You carried me in your womb all the while,
Every move of mine caused you pain,
yet your face always had a gentle smile.
You were the beacon of light guiding me to live,
Pampering me with love despite all your strife.
My first cries were heard, and I saw radiant smiles,
Thus, began my little journey of a million miles.
You held me close, you fed me out of your share,
I realized motherhood is something sacred and rare.
You helped me walk, you followed my every stumble,
You taught me to live, how to be noble.
I look back at those years and then I see,
Tears of gratitude fill my eyes and I smile with glee.
Like a candle eroding itself to spread the light,
You gave it all to make me wise and bright.
Now when I know the ways of this world,
You aren't with me, you left me out in the cold.

Your absence rips me apart at times,
Memories of you bring tears and sometimes smiles.
The lessons you taught will always hold a place,
In my heart and I will wade through life's unending maze.
Your love and warm touch are the things I miss,
Every single day, I blow you a gratitude-filled kiss.
I love you, Mom.

—*Giridhar Swaminath Jaded*

Racism

I wear a hoodie because my color is judged,

My friend wears shades to avoid being nudged.

From lonesome alleys to crowded streets,

I see smirks, grins, hideous eyes even behind expensive, exquisite, pleats.

Who I am or what's inside me, doesn't seem to matter,

Preconceived notions in people's minds kill me like a fish without water.

I wear a turban because I have this belief,

When I get off the bus, I hear loud sighs of relief.

I believe I am much more than the color of my skin,

But my freedom to some in this world is an unfathomable sin.

If I wear a white cap with tiny holes,

Imaginations will run amok, accusing me of destructive goals.

So, who are these people anyway?

The ones wearing these judgmental shades.

Are they so blind to not see someone for who they are?

Is it so hard to not blame everyone of a particular race and not go so far?

The world would be a lovely place without those judgmental shades,

The factories in the minds producing those
shades should be torn to shreds.

Only then will there be compassion in our hearts,

Where every person is seen for who they are and not
for their color, nationality, or body parts.

—*Giridhar Vineet Jaded*

The Depression Story

Being Depressed

Dreams can also seem like darkness,
Or rather an unending abyss.
When you are utterly depressed,
Every bit of emotion feels suppressed.
Every laugh around you can make your ears hurt,
You won't find joy at home or even at work.
Such is the web that depression weaves around you,
Making the sky look a fiery black when it's really pure blue.
Even compassion from loved ones is met with skepticism,
This world seems unreal, and you start hunting for another realm.

Clinging on to Hope

Hope is a wonderful thing, maybe the best of things,
It fills you with life – it can subtly grow invisible wings.
So, find that hope - that beautiful piece of rope,
Cling on to it as hard as you can grope.
Don't give up – it feels impossible to start with,
But slowly you will climb up garnering an otherworldly strength.
Depression is a demon that feeds on your inner fears,
Don't let it engulf you – don't let it drive you to tears.

<u>Beating the Depression Demon</u>

Sometimes all it takes is a willing mind,
Life also has people who are caring and kind.
Hold on to those threads and see yourself fly,
Be yourself - set fire to the past and set sights on your future a mile high.
One day when you look back and see that demon named Depression,
You will send a flying kiss its way and dismiss it into oblivion.
—*Giridhar Amruth Jaded*

Thank you for Reading.
KINDNESS IS FREE.
GOOD KARMA.